THE GOLDEN YEARS OF
MANCHESTER
PICTURE HOUSES

THE GOLDEN YEARS OF
MANCHESTER
PICTURE HOUSES

MEMORIES OF THE SILVER SCREEN 1900-1970

DEREK J. SOUTHALL

First published 2010

Reprinted 2012

The History Press
The Mill, Brimscombe Port
Stroud, Gloucestershire, GL5 2QG
www.thehistorypress.co.uk

ISBN 978 0 7524 4981 4

Typesetting and origination by The History Press
Printed and bound in Great Britain by
Marston Book Services Limited, Didcot

CONTENTS

INTRODUCTION

Cinema, compared with theatre, is a young art form, born at the end of the nineteenth century, peaking around 1940-50, and declining rapidly and extensively in the 1960s and '70s. Cinema mainly exists today in the cold characterless multiplexes on the outskirts of Britain's large cities and towns. But where are the cinemas which sprung into existence with the birth of film?

Manchester grew extensively in the first half of the twentieth century, incorporating many formerly independent towns. Concurrently cinema was gaining prominence as the leading form of entertainment. When cinema was silent, most areas of Manchester had picture houses; their number, with the arrival of sound, increased rapidly. Theatres, no longer drawing audiences, became cinemas and new cinemas were built, some of which were magnificent picture palaces.

The popularity of film as mass entertainment is easy to explain: easily accessible (a cinema was within walking distance of most homes); relatively cheap (a few pence a ticket and hardly a fortune for a whole family); it let its patrons experience a life they would otherwise never have the chance to know and see places they would never get to see; and took them away, however briefly, from the drudgery and toil of normal everyday existence. Moreover, in the lives of the glamorous people on the screen, it allowed them to see fleetingly what might have been. Cinemas were thronged with men, women and children, seeking escape and magic. On Saturday nights long queues would form outside the local picture houses – something unheard of nowadays; if you couldn't get into one, you hurried along to another. A child in the 1940s, I can still see the long queues that formed every Saturday outside the Workman's Hall and the Olympia – the two picture houses of my hometown in the Welsh valleys – from about 3 o'clock in the afternoon for the first showings, which began at 4 p.m. and 5 p.m.

There are great differences between present cinema showings and those in, say, 1950. Nowadays you book tickets in advance or turn up shortly before the programme commences. Cinemas are clean, tastefully lit, with perhaps twelve in the same building. You find your own way to a comfortable, backwards-sloping seat, with spaces in the arms for your drink, which accompanies the exorbitantly priced popcorn or hotdog you might have purchased on the way in. The programme begins with several exhortations, 'still time to buy your popcorn', 'don't let your sound effects [from mobile phones] ruin the show', 'absolutely no smoking'. Next, the

Adverts illustrating some of the cinemas in Manchester districts covered in this book.

adverts – slick, deafening, and off-putting – for everything from cars to beer. Then trailers for upcoming films, and finally the feature film. When the film is over, but the endless credits are still on the screen, the audience leaves the rather characterless building, which is identical to all the other cinemas in the complex, and all the other houses in that circuit, be it Cineworld, Odeon or AMG.

In 1950 'going to the pictures' was a very different experience. Seats were not generally bookable. To be sure of getting in you had to turn up early and take your place in the queue – along the front of the cinema and down the sides – either for the stalls seats (the cheapest) on one side of the box office, or the posher circle seats on the other. Many cinemas had a commissionaire to ensure that the queues stayed orderly. While you waited, there would be a buzz of anticipation; going to the pictures was an event. When the doors finally opened there was expectant chatter, while the queue began slowly to snake towards the box office. Your tickets bought ('two at 1s 3d please'), you made your way through the foyer doors into the cinema. An usherette collected the tickets and showed you to your seats. As the auditorium gradually filled up, it was amusing to watch latecomers trying to find three or four seats together.

A typical programme in the mid-twentieth century might include:

a. A newsreel – Paramount, Pathé, Movietone or Gaumont-British. This contained stories, each no more than a couple of minutes long, on politics, fashion, entertainments, or sporting events from around the world. The newsreel lasted about ten minutes.

b. Second feature (often called 'The Little Picture') – a western (with a star like Roy Rogers), a mystery (perhaps Charlie Chan), a comedy (Laurel and Hardy, Abbott and Costello), lasting sixty to seventy minutes. Because of a quota system, cinemas had to show a certain percentage of British films. The second feature was often a British B movie, from a company like Butchers or Hammer. Hollywood studios also made B movies.

c. Adverts – usually simple cards detailing a retailer or company, with only written information. Today's computer-generated special effects adverts were years in the future.

d. The trailers – previews of the pictures showing the following week. These were an art in themselves, showing scenes from the films (scenes sometimes cut from the finished film) and using words like 'Colossal', 'Magnificent', 'Stupendous' and 'Breath-taking'.

e. The feature film – lasting anything from seventy minutes to two hours, this was what the audience had really paid to see.

A cinema programme in the mid-twentieth century was real value for money. For a shilling (5p) you got around three hours' entertainment. No audience could complain of being short-changed. Most cinemas changed their programmes midweek: one programme playing Monday, Tuesday and Wednesday; a different programme on Thursday, Friday and

Queuing up for the pictures, a Saturday night ritual – almost – in the 1940s and '50s.

Saturday. Programmes usually played for a week in the big city picture palaces, and might be retained for a second week or longer if the film proved a box office draw. Sunday cinema was not common until after the Second World War; the films shown were generally old movies, in very poor, hacked-about prints.

The only significant variation in cinema programming from the coming of the talkies until the late 1960s was the double bill programmes. A studio would programme two of its films together, a western perhaps and a musical, or a comedy and a thriller. Both films, each lasting about eighty minutes, featured the studio's stars. Universal did this most frequently. A typical Universal double bill programme in the 1950s was *Female on the Beach*, starring Joan Crawford and Jeff Chandler, a black-and-white melodrama, and *This Island Earth*, a sci-fi film in Technicolor. Such programmes often proved more popular than much-publicised 'big' pictures.

The release pattern for films in the 1940s-50s was very different from today. A new film would open in London's West End and play for three weeks. A week or so later it played circuit cinemas in major cities. There were three main circuits until the late 1950s – Odeon and Gaumont, both part of the Rank Organisation, and ABC; they had a monopoly on new films. The smaller independent cinemas in most towns could not show new movies until they had played the major cities. A film shown in London and major centres in January might not reach places like Levenshulme or Miles Platting until August or September. The current release pattern – new pictures opening throughout the country on the same day – is much better.

A typical Universal double bill from 1952. A black-and-white melodrama and a Technicolor western.

Britain's two most popular film magazines in the 1930–60 period.

Picture-going in the 1930–60 period was backed up by widespread advertising, with posters outside each cinema, and on hoardings on the streets, shops, gable-end walls and many other locations. People, as eager to read about their film idols as to see them on screen, bought two film magazines – *Picturegoer* and *Picture Show* – in vast numbers. These contained film reviews, star stories and pictures, adverts for new films, and casting news. The author was an avid reader of both.

In 1948 the cinema page of the *Manchester Evening News* listed more than 100 cinemas in Manchester's city centre and outer districts. Openshaw, with seven cinemas, had the highest number; most places had two or three, often in the same street and occasionally next door to each other. Cinema audiences peaked around that year. By 1970 most of those cinemas had closed, been demolished and the site redeveloped, or had changed from showing films to holding bingo sessions. Some became clubs, some churches; one even became a funeral director's premises. In 2010 not one of the cinemas from 1948 still exists. A few of the buildings do, mostly in a derelict state. Almost all traces of the early and mid-twentieth century's most popular form of entertainment have vanished; few records of the buildings, which played such a vital part in social life for more than sixty years, remain.

This book is an attempt to chronicle the growth and decline of the picture house in Manchester and its districts, and to give a glimpse into an almost vanished past. It has been written with much affection, by someone who all his life has loved movies and the places where they are shown. Most of that life has been spent in the North West, and many happy hours in the picture houses of Manchester and its suburbs. If the book serves to show today's audiences what 'going to the pictures' meant to their parents and grandparents, I will be well content. I should note finally here, that the personal memories included in this book are as people remember things, and we do not always remember with historical accuracy.

Derek J. Southall, 2010

Author's Note

The 'Manchester' of the title is before Greater Manchester was born in the 1970s – the area covered here includes city centre Manchester along with the districts of Ancoats, Ardwick, Beswick, Blackley, Bradford, Burnage, Cheetham, Chorlton-cum-Hardy, Chorlton-on-Medlock, Clayton, Collyhurst, Didsbury, Fallowfield, Gorton, Harpurhey, Hulme, Levenshulme, Longsight, Miles Platting, Moss Side, Moston, Newton Heath, Northenden, Openshaw, Rusholme, Whalley Range, Withington and Wythenshawe.

Acknowledgements

I would like to put on record my thanks to the many people who helped me with this book, especially everyone who spoke to me about the cinemas and loaned me precious personal pictures. My thanks also to the staff of Manchester Central Library local studies/archive department, especially Jane Parr, for their invaluable help and for the use of some of their photographs; and to the Cinema Theatre Association (CTA), the Tony Moss Collection and especially the CTA archivist, Clive Polden. Finally, but by no means least, my book, a real labour of love, would never have happened without the unstinting help of my friend Graham Chard, who ferried me many miles around the great city of Manchester to find and to take pictures of the cinema buildings which remain, and who helped this computer-illiterate author with the pictures and preparation of the book.

ONE

ARDWICK, ANCOATS, BESWICK AND BRADFORD

Ardwick, Ancoats, Beswick and Bradford border Manchester city centre – so closely intertwined that it is difficult to work out where one ends and another begins. In the golden years of cinema, the 1920s to the 1960s, Ardwick had three cinemas and a theatre which, briefly, became a cinema. The oldest was the Coliseum, on the corner of Dolphin Street/Dolphin Place, just off Hyde Road and almost hidden by Ardwick Empire Theatre.

A huge barn of a place, with seating for nearly 2,000 people, the Coliseum had previously been an ice rink. Doreen Thompson recalls: 'My dad was doorman at the Coliseum and the first film I ever saw there was *Bambi*.' There seem to be conflicting views about what the Coliseum was like inside. Megan Neesom remembers 'a huge place, but a bug hut. The attendants used to go round during the performance to spray disinfectant to kill the bugs.' Roy Pennell recalls it differently, however: 'Although the Coliseum was in a poor area, it was comfortable and clean, popular with locals.' Roy also recollects that when he was a young boy with little money, in the 1930s, three or four lads each gave a penny to a friend, who would buy a 3*d* admission ticket. Once inside he'd open a side door to let his mates in. The usherettes turned a blind eye, aware that money was scarce. The Coliseum lasted until the late 1940s. The last film shown there was *The Birth of a Baby* – a birth followed quickly by a death, when the Coliseum closed in the spring of 1949 and was later demolished.

Opposite the Coliseum, across Hyde Road, was the Ardwick Picture Theatre, which opened on 4 November 1920, advertised as 'Manchester's largest and finest cinema'. In the early 1930s, after it was adapted for talkies, it became part of the ABC circuit, remaining so for the next ten years, up to the beginning of the war. Megan Neesom remembers the Ardwick, which could seat 1,600 people, as 'a very nice picture house, always very clean'. On the night of 11 March 1941, German bombers targeted the Ardwick area. Seven bombs fell around Ardwick Green; one scored a direct hit on the Ardwick Picture Theatre. The building was destroyed and the site was afterwards used for emergency water storage (EWS). Elsie Swainson worked at the Apollo during the war and remembers that, 'When you looked out from the staff room at the Apollo towards the EWS, it looked like an inviting swimming pool.' Evidence of the last film ever

Composite advert (not all for the same years) for Ardwick, Ancoats, Beswick and Bradford picture houses.

shown at the Ardwick remained for many months – a poster for *The Westerner* starring Gary Cooper was left flapping in the wind.

Twelve months before the outbreak of the Second World War a new picture house opened on Ardwick Green. The Apollo, opened on 29 August 1938 by the Deputy Lord Mayor of Manchester and the popular film star Margaret Lockwood, was a huge picture palace, fit to rival its two competitors, the Gaumont and the Paramount on Oxford Street, Manchester. The foyer stretched along the cinema's frontage on Stockport Road. From it you entered a vast auditorium, with stalls and a circle with steeply-raked seating, and side walls decorated with hundreds of shapes – like figure sixes laid on their sides.

The Apollo was a very popular venue for cinema-goers. It had a café, though Jean Wheeldon, who worked near Ardwick Green in her teens, says, 'We couldn't afford the café, but we took sandwiches and often went to the Apollo to the pictures after work.' Betty Wade recalls: 'The Apollo was a lovely place. It was ahead of its time and it always felt very posh.' The new cinema served as a first-run house, often sharing its programmes with the Regal Twins on Oxford Road. When the Ardwick was destroyed by a German bomb, the ABC circuit cast around for a new venue in the area, settling on the Apollo. In the spring of 1943, ABC took over the Apollo from the original owners, R.C. Roy and Anglo-Scottish Theatres Ltd. Elsie Swainson, who worked as an usherette at the Apollo for more than four years in the early 1940s, recalls:

The Coliseum, Ardwick. (Courtesy of Cinema Theatre Association, Tony Moss Collection)

The Ardwick Picture Theatre, in the early 1930s. (Courtesy of Cinema Theatre Association, Tony Moss Collection)

The Apollo in 2009, just before a concert and much as it would have looked when it was a picture house.

Staff of the Apollo, Ardwick, in 1943 when it was showing *Yankee Doodle Dandy*.

The manageress was Mrs Hilda Topping. The cinema had beautiful thick carpets throughout as well as a lovely restaurant and ballroom. In the interval an organ ascended from beneath the screen and organist Sidney Gustard entertained patrons for fifteen minutes. The Apollo kept films for one week; the only one it retained was *Yankee Doodle Dandy*, which starred James Cagney in his Oscar-winning role.

The Apollo was shaped like a letter L and, in the foot of the L, on Hyde Road, was the ballroom, which was damaged when the Germans bombed the area. Elsie remembers that during the war, after the evacuation from Dunkirk, returning soldiers were sent all over the country. Some were housed in the Apollo and many were injured, all dirty, and some minus shoes and top clothes.

Films continued to be shown at the Apollo for more than forty years. It was, for a long time, ABC's flagship cinema in Manchester and its Saturday morning ABC Minors' Matinees were very popular with many of the people interviewed for this book. The location on Ardwick Green, on several major roads and bus routes, made it a popular venue for a night out. In 1979 the owners (by then Maximus Investments, later the Apollo Group), took the decision to build a mini cinema beneath the Apollo's dance hall and to use the main auditorium of the cinema as a concert venue. The mini cinema lasted little more than a year, but the concert venue still exists in 2010, and stars as diverse as Johnny Mathis and the Beatles have played there. One of the city's few surviving cinema buildings, the Apollo has now been in existence for some seventy years — not bad going for a venue that opened with George Formby in *I See Ice*.

When I first came to the North West in 1959 I frequently travelled from Ashton-under-Lyne to Manchester to visit the city centre cinemas. The quickest bus route was the 213, which went along Ashton New Road into Manchester through the Ancoats district. There is still a bus stop at the Manchester end of Ashton Old Road, and I remember that, when the bus stopped there, from the top deck I was able to see the building which had once been the Don cinema. This small picture house opened just before the outbreak of the First World War. It had no balcony/circle, but Harry Bramwell remembers that the ground floor sloped steeply from the front to the back, so that people in each row were higher than those in the row in front of them. 'If you walked from the front to the back of the Don, your legs ached,' Harry comments. Derek Blinston recollects, 'The dear seats were 9*d*. Kids paid 2*d*. On Saturday mornings we used to go to the Don to watch the likes of *Hop-along Cassidy*.' The Don eventually became part of the ABC circuit. Terry O'Grady remembers:

The first film I ever saw at the Don was *The Wizard of Oz*. The cinema used to advertise the week's offering on either side of the entrance — Monday, Tuesday and Wednesday one side, Thursday, Friday and Saturday on the other. However, when the MGM picture *King Solomon's Mines* played there, a new billboard was installed above the entrance.

Eddie Pickerill got his first job — as a trainee projectionist — at the Don when he left school at fourteen. He remembers the chief projectionist was a Frenchman named Jules. Eddie was responsible for putting the spools of the newsreel back into their containers when the news had been shown at the Don, and running up the hill with them to the Tower cinema. The Don and the Tower were both ABC cinemas and shared the newsreel. The Don lasted until February

1958, when it closed after the final showing of *The Prince and the Showgirl*, starring Marilyn Monroe and Laurence Olivier – surely the only time two such glittering stars closed a cinema! The building, used in succeeding years for industrial purposes, was eventually demolished. Today there's just a patch of grass there.

The Tower cinema, opened in 1913 and part of the Circuit Cinema group, was up the hill from the Don, on Piercy Street. Harry Bramwell recalls it as 'a bug hut, though, to be fair, it was small and clean.' Later it was taken over by ABC. It had a small balcony, and, as Derek Blinston recalls, 'wooden benches instead of seats at the front of the stalls.' Derek remembers sneaking in, when he was just eleven years old, to watch films about Auschwitz, though he recalls that the manager, Johnny Morris – whom the kids called Johnny Oxo – was always on to them if they sneaked in. He also recollects getting old cinema posters from the Tower to burn on the kids' Guy Fawkes bonfire – how much would those posters be worth today? The Tower lasted through the boom years of cinema but finally closed at the end of May 1952. The final film shown there was a B movie, *Miraculous Journey*, supported by *The Big Fight* starring Joe Palooka. The building was eventually pulled down.

Butler Street runs from the top of Beswick Street to Oldham Road. In 1912 a picture house called the Electric opened on Butler Street, near its junction with Oldham Road. In 1931, after the installation of sound, it became the Butler Electric Theatre, remaining so until 1940. In December of that year, when the Luftwaffe bombed Manchester, the Ancoats area suffered considerable damage and the Butler was among the buildings so badly damaged it had to be demolished. However, after the war, the rebuilt picture house reopened in March 1950, with a new name, the Savoy, though people in the area continued to call it the Butler. The manager then was Mr R. Scholes. Edna King, who worked at Shaw and Jardine Fine Cotton Spinners on Butler Street, recalls that 'One afternoon a group of us girls decided to give work a miss and go to the pictures. We went to the Butler. But, would you believe, the foreman from work came in and dragged us all out back to work.'

Unfortunately, the Butler's life as a cinema was not very long, since it closed in April of 1956, after a mere six years. Avril Craig lived with her mother and older brother Alan and their grandmother in Miles Platting. Alan used to go down Oldham Road to visit the Butler. He said to Avril, then seven or eight, 'It costs 3*d* to go in – 2*d* for the ticket and 1*d* for the hammer.' 'What do you need a hammer for?' was her reply. 'To kill the bugs, of course,' Alan responded.

Ancoats had one other picture house, which had also opened shortly before the outbreak of the First World War. It was on Palmerston Street, which runs between Ashton New Road and Great Ancoats Street, and was called the Ancoats Picturedrome. Jim Callander, who has lived in the area all his life, recalls that kids called the picture house the 'Penny Palmy' after the price of the cheapest seats. The building was near to Ardwick Lads' Club. The Ancoats Picturedrome vanishes from records after 1940. Since the Ancoats area, including Palmerston Street, was very badly damaged by German bombs in December of 1940, it seems likely that the picture house was among the casualties, too badly damaged to be reconstructed.

The Beswick and Bradford areas of Manchester are nowadays part of Eastlands, which is occupied mainly by the City of Manchester Stadium and a very large Asda store. Beswick, on the north side of Ashton New Road, had one small picture house, called the Mosley. Opened on Stott Street in 1914, as the Mosley Picture Palace, it was owned for much of its lifetime

The Don, Beswick, in the early 1930s. (Courtesy of Cinema Theatre Association archive)

The Tower, Ancoats, 1936. (Courtesy of Cinema Theatre Association, Tony Moss Collection)

Butler Street with the Savoy cinema in 1962, six years after it closed. (Courtesy of Manchester Archives and Local Studies, Central Library)

The premises of Diplomac & Co. raincoat manufacturers, previously the Mosley cinema.

by Mrs M.W. Watts. Terry Rourke remembers that the Mosley 'operated rather differently from other local picture houses, probably because it was privately owned. Where continuous performances were the norm in most houses, the Mosley operated a policy of two separate performances each night.'

It provided film entertainment for residents of the area for almost half a century, before finally closing its doors in February 1961, after the final showing of a Walt Disney programme, *Kidnapped* and *White Wilderness*. Sheila Fitzpatrick, who went to Saturday morning pictures at the Mosley, remembers:

> … a small cinema in the midst of many little streets, with a corner shop on every corner. On Saturday mornings we queued up at the side and we paid 6*d*. The boys used to fire peas or fling orange peel at each other, and we would hiss when the villains appeared. The manager would often stop the film to tell us off.

A photograph of Stott Street, taken in 1962, shows just one building remaining, a rainwear manufacturer called Diplomac & Co. The building is too much like an old picture house for it to be anything but the Mosley in a new guise. Today the whole area has altered; where the Mosley once stood is now a car park for football fans. Eddie Pickerill, though, in common with others brought up in the area, remembers the picture house with affection: 'We used to queue up outside in all weathers to get in for 1*d*. We kids called it the Penny Crush.'

Across Ashton New Road, in the Bradford area of the city, stood the most luxurious of the cinemas in the area (until the Apollo Ardwick opened). On the left-hand side of Ashton New Road, going towards the city, the Royal Picturedrome (between Rhodes Street and Parker Street) started its life in 1914, but was knocked down in 1930 and rebuilt on a more ambitious scale. The rebuilt picture house was called the New Royal. In 1939 it became ABC's third and most prestigious picture house in the area, more up-market than the Don and the Tower. Terry O'Grady says:

My wife lived in an adjoining street and the New Royal was where we did much of our courting. There were steps up to the entrance and the pay box was situated in the centre of the entrance. The New Royal had stalls and a balcony. The seats at the back of the stalls were beneath the balcony, and more intimate for courting couples.

Geoff Logan recalls the New Royal as 'a posh place. I once saw comedian Arthur Haynes make a personal appearance there.' The New Royal showed Pathé News in its programmes. It shared the newsreel with another ABC cinema, the Queen's on Ashton Old Road, so reels of film had to be ferried between the two cinemas, whose programmes were arranged to facilitate this. The New Royal had a longer life as a picture house than any other in the area, providing entertainment in comfortable and pleasant surroundings for more than half a century, before finally closing its doors on Saturday, 25 January 1969, when the last film shown there was the Yul Brynner actioner *Villa Rides*. No trace of the building remains today.

Sheila Fitzpatrick has a vivid memory of the New Royal:

I lived in a street at the side of the New Royal. It was a beautiful picture house; the interior walls had paintings of nursery rhymes in circles. There were steps up to the pay box and on either side of the entrance were showcases advertising the current film and next week's attraction. There were always usherettes to show you to your seats and keep order, and during the interval there was a Lyons Maid ice cream lady who sold lovely orange lollipops.

Terence Nixon also has a memory of the New Royal. If a message needed to be given to a patron in a picture house, the practice was to scratch the message onto a slide and project it over the film. One night in the 1960s, Terence was in the audience of the New Royal when a message appeared on the screen asking that any relations of Lesley Ann Downey who were in the audience should contact the cinema manager. Terence learned later that Lesley Ann had become one of the child victims of the Moors murderers.

TWO

CLAYTON, MILES PLATTING AND NEWTON HEATH

Ashton New Road winds its way from just inside the Manchester boundary through Clayton into Droylsden. One of Manchester's more impressive picture houses, built when the talkies made going to the pictures hugely popular, was to be found in Clayton from 1930 onwards. The Carlton Super Cinema stood on the south side of Ashton New Road, next door to Mayne's Bus and Coach Garage. It opened on 7 July 1930 and remained there, an imposing landmark, for more than seventy years, though its life as a picture house ended in 1964. Because it was used for variety shows as well as films, the Carlton had a stage and six dressing rooms. It also boasted a café, a popular meeting place. Sheila Fitzpatrick, born and brought up half a mile down the road in Bradford, ventured to the Carlton as she got older since it was within easy walking distance.

Sheila recollects that, if you wanted to go to the second house at the Carlton on a Saturday night, it was essential to book your seats – otherwise you could not get in. A popular venue during its cinema lifetime, the Carlton's demise as a picture house was sudden and unexpected. Adverts for the week of 24 February 1964 promised Paul Newman and Joanne Woodward in *A New Kind of Love*, but also announced that films would play in the evenings from 5.30 p.m. with bingo on Sunday at 3 p.m. and Monday to Wednesday at 2.30 p.m. Adverts for the following week, however, announced the start of the Carlton Bingo Club, with two sessions daily. Paul Newman, it seems, was no match for 'Eyes down'. The Carlton continued with bingo until it closed. It remained on the site, shut and derelict, into the twenty-first century when, unannounced and without ceremony, the building was demolished in 2006.

Oldham Road makes its way north-east from central Manchester to the destination for which it is named, passing through Miles Platting and Newton Heath. Heavily built-up areas, with many working-class families, the two districts were perfect for the siting of picture houses, when cinema became the mass entertainment of the early twentieth century. Oldham Road was the location of one of Manchester's finest theatres. Opened in April 1896 on the north side of Oldham Road in Miles Platting, just a few minutes from Manchester city centre, was the Royal Osborne Theatre. It was owned, in common with several other local theatres, by William

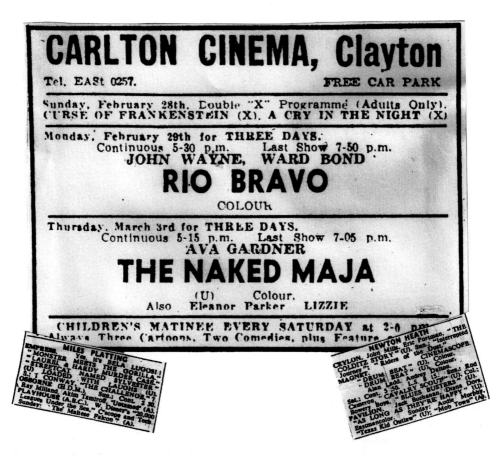

Composite advert for Clayton, Miles Platting and Newton Heath picture houses, 1950s.

Henry Broadhead. The majority of the most famous entertainers of the early twentieth century, including Marie Lloyd and Charlie Chaplin, graced its stage. Irene Young recalls that, after the Osborne became a picture house, events still took place on stage – one of which was a competition (for boys) to find out who could best imitate Charlie Chaplin. The theatre was also used for circus performances. Avril Craig lived with her mother and brother in her grandmother's house around the corner from the Osborne.

> My mother loved to tell the story of how, one day, when she was sitting in the kitchen of Grandmother's house, the door opened and a lion walked in, followed by his trainer, who had him on a leash. They were part of a circus which was at the Osborne that week, and the trainer was taking the lion for a walk through the streets near the theatre.

The Osborne became a picture house in 1935. Although the seating was reduced by almost 200, to 1,300, when the Osborne was converted, it was never ideal for seeing films. 'If you sat at the back of the stalls,' remembers Irene Young, 'you could not see the top of the screen.' Avril Craig, recalling happy times at the Osborne, says:

The Carlton, Clayton, in the mid-1950s.

I used to go with my older brother on a Saturday. The seats at the front were long benches, with metal back rests covered in red plush. We kids had to sit in straight rows at the front. When the lights went out, we used to crawl under the seats to get to better seats at the back. My brother and I once went to the Osborne and the lady in the pay box said, 'I'm sorry lad. You have to be sixteen to come in to this film.' My brother, who had red hair and was just twelve, said, 'I am sixteen.'

'If you are sixteen, I'm sixty,' the pay box lady responded. 'I'm not arguing,' said my cheeky brother. The lady left the pay box and chased him up the street.

The Osborne, which eventually became part of the HDM circuit, continued as a picture house into the late 1950s. At 2 a.m. on the morning of Monday, 20 October 1958, a passing policeman noticed flames in the building and raised the alarm. Fire had broken out in the projection box and the fire crews could not save the building, which was very badly damaged and never reopened as a cinema. Its last film, somewhat ironically, was *Hell's Outpost*. The building appears to have been demolished, though another Osborne theatre – a venue for pop concerts – replaced it and still survives in a very dilapidated state.

Further along Oldham Road there was another large picture house, the Empress. Opened about 1908 as the Empress Electric Theatre, it had 1,200 seats, and, though for a time it belonged to the Broadhead circuit, for most of its life it was an independent picture house. Colette Mealing, born and brought up in Miles Platting, used to go to the Empress with her dad, and remembers seeing her first cartoon feature, Walt Disney's *Lady and the Tramp* there in 1959. 'The Empress,' says Colette, 'was a large building, but a rather scruffy place. People in the area would often ask, "Are you coming to the flea pit?" when they meant the Empress.'

Derelict Osborne theatre, 2009.

The Empress picture house, Miles Platting, shortly before fire destroyed it. (Courtesy of Frank Rhodes)

Colette Mealing (*née* Morton) with her dad, Frederick – frequent visitors to the Empress, Miles Platting.

The picture house, which Irene Young recalls as 'A poor substitute for the Osborne and the Playhouse,' was nevertheless a popular place, since it stayed in business on Oldham Road until August 1961, when it changed from films to bingo. The last picture shown there was the horror movie *13 Ghosts*, supported by *The Screaming Mimi*. In the 1990s the building became a warehouse, and was then left empty and derelict for some time. As a listed building, one would have expected work to be done to preserve it, but in June 2006 a fire broke out in the Empress and the building was destroyed. The fact that it had been a listed building caused questions to be raised about the cause of the fire, but the damage was done, and another cinema landmark had disappeared.

The people of Miles Platting were well catered for in terms of picture houses, with a third large venue on Oldham Road – the Playhouse, opened in the silent movie days and providing film entertainment there for half a century. It was, recalls Colette Mealing, 'a massive building, at the junction of Hulme Hall Road and Oldham Road. It had a dome, and inside there were stalls and a balcony.' The cinema could seat nearly 1,900 people, and tradition has it that it was built by the original owner for his daughter's twenty-first birthday. Irene Young told me:

> I used to go to stay with an aunt in Moston. I would get the bus back along Oldham Road and get off outside the Playhouse, where my mother was waiting to take me to see whatever picture was showing. The Playhouse was a bit of a flea pit.

An independent cinema at first, the Playhouse became part of the ABC circuit in 1945 and remained so until the end of its life as a cinema. Colette Mealing has vivid memories of going there with her girl friends in the 1960s to see all the musicals starring Elvis Presley.

The Playhouse lasted longer than most cinemas; ABC closed it on 9 June 1970, when the film showing was the horror picture *Scream and Scream Again*, supported by *Hell's Angels '69*. For the next fifteen years or so the building was used as a bingo hall, closing in 1986, after which it stood empty for a decade or more until finally being demolished in 1998.

The Osborne, the Empress and the Playhouse could cater for 4,500 patrons. But, from 1912 until the mid-1940s, Miles Platting also boasted a smaller picture house, not far from the Playhouse. The Popular Picture Palace in Wilson Street was a very modest place. Irene Young remembers:

> It was called 'The Pop' by the locals. It never got the big films first – they went to the Empress, the Playhouse or the Osborne. But if you missed a film in one of those and your friends told you how good it was, you knew you could catch up with it at The Pop, where programmes played for only two days.

The people of Miles Platting who were interviewed for this book all had very affectionate memories of the picture houses of the area. Avril Craig, who lived in Miles Platting for some years with her mother and brother, loved going to the pictures but was always on tenterhooks in case her mum would not get home from work in time. When she was just nine years old she penned this little poem to her mother:

> The night is growing darker now,
> The place is growing drear.
> The picture house is open now.
> Are we going, mother dear?

Playhouse picture house, Miles Platting, in 1968. (Courtesy of Holme Cinema Theatre Association archive)

Leaving Miles Platting to enter Newton Heath, Thorp Road is on your left. Not far along Thorp Road, on your right, stands a large building, used today as a bathroom wholesaler's. The building was originally the Ceylon cinema, which had an interesting history. Ceylon Street runs behind and parallel with Oldham Road, and at right angles to Thorp Road. Newton Heath Congregational Church was on Ceylon Street in the nineteenth century. The church, struggling for members in the years before the First World War, eventually decided to sell the premises for £1,000. The new owner converted the building to a picture house, which he called the Ceylon. The pillars of the old church were apparently retained without obstructing anyone's view of the screen. The picture house on Ceylon Street stayed in business until 1938, when a new cinema opened on Thorp Road, taking the Ceylon name. The building on Ceylon Street became a dance hall. John Coleclough, who played in the band there, remembers it as a very large building and recalls how sad everyone was when the manager told them the dance hall was closing and would reopen as a bingo hall. That happened in 1962, and the bingo hall was there until the building was destroyed by fire in 1992. John was only a boy when the Ceylon cinema on Thorp Road opened. He says:

> The Ceylon's main entrance, where you got tickets for the dearer seats, was on Thorp Road, but if you couldn't afford those seats you had to go to the back of the cinema to buy tickets for the cheaper seats. I remember going to the Ceylon with my mother, and can still recall how she laughed hysterically at the antics of Danny Kaye in *Up in Arms*.

John also recalls how, as an older child, he would go to the Ceylon on his own. Some films could only be seen by children if they were accompanied by an adult. John would walk along

Ceylon Newton Heath 2009, no longer a picture house but a bathroom outfitter's.

THE MAGNET CINEMA

CHURCH STREET · NEWTON HEATH

Directorate: C. GREENHALGH, A. SNAPE, A. E. WRIGHT, J. HOWARD
Secretary: G. BRIAN SNAPE

Souvenir Programme

PREMIER PERFORMANCE
December, 1938

The cover of the souvenir programme for the opening of the Magnet, Newton Heath.

An artist's impression of the Magnet, Newton Heath.

the queue, looking for a man or woman with a kind face, and hold out his ticket money, pleading, 'Will you take me in please?' It never failed. The Ceylon, which had 800 seats, stayed in business until May 1960, when it closed after the final showing of *Tommy the Toreador* and *Up in Smoke*.

Newton Heath is an area rich in cinema history. In the very centre of the town, on Old Church Street, from 1938 on, it was possible to see a very unusual sight (at least outside the major cities). Two picture houses were in business next door to each other. The older one, the Pavilion, had opened in 1915. It could seat 1,000 people, but seems to have been something of a bug hut. John Coleclough remembers going there to see all the Old Mother Riley comedy films, and the Tarzan pictures which Johnny Weissmuller made. He also sheds interesting light on what picture-going was like during the war:

> If ever a newsreel had pictures of British planes dropping bombs in German cities, everybody in the audience cheered and clapped, as they did if the newsreel showed pictures of King George VI and Queen Elizabeth. The National Anthem was played at the end of every performance; everyone stayed and everyone stood up for it.

Joan Knibbs, who was born and brought up in the area, got a job at Ferranti when she left school. She had a part-time evening job too, as an usherette at the Pavilion.

I used to rush home from Ferranti, grab a sandwich, then hurry to the Pavilion. I was an usherette there and also sold ice cream during the interval. I hated that tray full of ice creams that I had to carry around my neck. Once the interval was over we were allowed to sit at the back of the picture house and watch the rest of the programme. My boyfriend used to come and he would sit and watch the picture, then he'd walk me home. The money was useful; it wasn't very much, but it helped me to save up for holidays.

The Pavilion entertained Newton Heath people for nearly half a century, finally closing its doors on Sunday, 3 May 1964 after a showing of two Universal films, *This Earth is Mine*, starring Rock Hudson and Jean Simmons, and an Audie Murphy western *No Name on the Bullet*.

In 1938 the Pavilion got a new, and much grander, neighbour when the Magnet Super Cinema opened right next door. The opening, rather tactless, publicity cannot have done much to allay any fears the Pavilion management might have:

> In the district where the new Magnet cinema has been placed there has, for a long time, been a need for a new, up-to-date place of entertainment … the Newton Heath district has not yet been catered for by the type of cinema such as we now present.

The management also announced a different Saturday matinee policy: 'We are NOT going to run children's matinees. There are over 100 cinemas in the suburbs of Manchester and practically all of them run children's matinees.' The Magnet would run matinees for grown-ups. Then, chauvinistically and politically incorrect by today's standards: 'Married men should be in sympathy with this policy, for they can pay for their wives to go to the matinees on Saturday afternoons and sneak out to the football match much easier.' Prices in the new picture palace ranged from 1*s* in the Grand Lounge to 4*d* in the stalls, and from 6*d* to 3*d* at matinees. Mildred Leigh, who was born and brought up in Newton Heath, says of the Magnet:

Auditorium of the Magnet, Newton Heath.

It was a plush cinema on a par with Manchester's picture palaces. It was very warm and comfortable. The screen curtains had pictures of gondolas in Venice on them. There was a large foyer, with glass display cases and photos of popular stars and ads for next week's pictures. The manager wore a dark suit and a black bow tie, which made him stand out.

The Magnet and the Pavilion managed to co-exist side-by-side for some twenty-four years. Surprisingly the Magnet was first to close, on 30 June 1962, when the film was *One, Two, Three*, supported by *Incident in an Alley*. The building became a supermarket and was eventually demolished. The Pavilion, which followed the Magnet two years later, was also pulled down and now a Lidl supermarket stands on the site.

POSTER MAN

In cinema's heyday, a long-forgotten industry flourished in cinema's shadow – the business of poster writing. Every cinema exhibited outdoor posters, often one each side of the entrance. These were called 'oils' and could range from 5ft to 50ft long. Since most picture houses changed programmes midweek, and had a different show on Sunday, poster-making flourished. Manchester's two largest poster-making companies were Gordon's Publicity and ADS (Art Display Services), each employing about 100 staff. Cyril Walker worked for Gordon's:

Oils was my domain. We worked in groups, almost conveyor belt fashion. One guy pinned sheets of white paper on long wooden benches, followed by a foreman ruling lines by walking backwards with a pencil on the end of his 3ft ruler, the other end following the edge of the bench. Another guy put in Monday, Tuesday and Wednesday, another the star's name, another the film's title and yet another 'Full supporting programme'. The pins were out, the sheets put under the table to dry (which didn't take long because the special ink was thinned with petrol, which evaporated quickly – most of it into our clothes!) Because so many posters were needed each week, speed was of the essence. The speed of the production line was down to precision-made one-stroke brushes and the aid of a finger stick to guide your brush in a straight line. I served in the navy as a telegraphist. When I returned to Gordon's, one of my regular jobs was the Odeon Derby. I had a mate in Derby and kept in touch by putting a border in Morse code around the Odeon poster.

THREE

COLLYHURST, HARPURHEY, MOSTON AND BLACKLEY

Collyhurst and Harpurhey lie between Oldham Road and Rochdale Road. When cinema was the most popular form of mass entertainment, Collyhurst had four picture houses, all situated on Rochdale Road. The Gem Electric Theatre, opened in 1912, changed its name to the Regent when talkies arrived. Owned by Mostyn Sereno, it was a small house with seating for just 600 patrons. Weekday performances were continuous, with matinees on Mondays and Thursdays, but on Saturdays there were two separate shows. Seat prices were very modest. The Regent was the first of the Collyhurst picture houses to yield to the threat of television, closing at the end of June 1956, but reopening soon after as a bingo hall. Ken Martin remembers the Gem/Regent, along with the Plaza/Astor as 'two bug huts'.

The Gem/Regent was adjacent to Scropton Street, near the junction of Queen's Road and Rochdale Road. A little way down Rochdale Road, towards Manchester, was the Astor, which opened in 1913 as the Queen's Park Picturedrome. It underwent a third name change when it became the Plaza, but in 1953 it changed again, becoming the New Astor, at which point it began advertising in the *Manchester Evening News*. It lasted only six years under that name, finally closing in 1959. The Gem/Regent and the Astor were owned by two Sereno brothers. Robert Birchenough knew both picture houses and recalls, 'The Plaza/Astor was built over the railway line which comes out on Queen's Road. When a train went by the cinema shook and steam came in.' He also remembers the Plaza's odd but generous way of doing business: 'It cost 2*d* to get into the Plaza. If you only had a penny, Mr Sereno gave you the other penny so you could buy your ticket. That way you got in and he at least made a penny.'

If you continued down Rochdale Road you would, in the early years of the twentieth century, have come to an ice rink. A picture house called the Palace opened next door to the ice rink in 1927, under the same manager, Bertram E. Wake. A prominent position on a main road kept the Palace, which could seat some 700 paying customers, in business into the mid-1950s, when it closed to become a bingo hall. When the bingo hall closed in the 1970s, the building was used for music gigs. It became the Electric Circus, and Joy Division made their first public appearance there. It lasted a few years in that capacity but then closed and was eventually pulled down.

Composite advert for Collyhurst, Harpurhey, Moston and Blackley picture houses.

Collyhurst's fourth picture house was, by far, its largest and most luxurious – a picture palace compared to the others. The Rivoli, owned by Ben Kanter, opened just before Christmas 1937. A 'red-brick building', it had a prominent position on Rochdale Road, 'down a dip between Queen's Road and Collyhurst Street' – to quote Ken Martin – and quickly established itself as a very popular venue for a night out, giving its patrons a touch of the luxury which was missing from their everyday lives in austere post-war Britain. The Rivoli could seat almost 1,200 people, twice as many as any other Collyhurst picture house, and was quickly a landmark in the area. Soon after the end of the Second World War, the Rivoli underwent a change of ownership. Ben Kanter sold the cinema to the Essoldo circuit and it was renamed the Essoldo, a name which it kept until the end of its days. It lasted longer than many picture houses, outliving all three of its Collyhurst neighbours, surviving until 5 February 1966 and closing after the final showing of the Peter O'Toole film *Lord Jim*. It did reopen for bingo – a sad fate for what had been a lovely picture house – but the building was finally demolished.

Harpurhey, Collyhurst's neighbour, boasted only one cinema – at least according to the *Manchester Evening News*. There are those, however, born and bred in Harpurhey, who might lay claim to the Empire on Factory Lane and the Palladium on Rochdale Road. The *Manchester Evening News*, under Harpurhey, advertised only the Princess, on Conran Street. The Princess Picture Hall opened in 1913. With seating for 795 patrons, it provided film entertainment for Harpurhey residents for some forty-five years. Maureen Hodson often went there with her mother and, like many local people, refers to the picture house as 'The Prinny'. In common with many other picture houses, the Princess was hit by falling audiences in the mid-1950s, as television became more prevalent. It held on until just before Christmas 1958, when it was showing a double bill of two second features, *Them Nice Americans* and *Stronghold*. It closed after the last showing but the building stood on the site for thirty-eight years, until destroyed by fire in 1994. It is now the site of Conran Street market.

Moston is Collyhurst's neighbour to the east. For many years it boasted a picture house called the Moston Imperial Palace, or MIP for short. Brian Lynch describes it as 'anything but a palace – a flea pit in fact'. It had no balcony, but the seats – some 1,000 of them – sloped upwards from the front, the most expensive being at the very back. Irene Young recalls that, 'If you were sitting at the side you could only see three quarters of the screen.' Brian Lynch reminisces:

I used to go on Saturday mornings to get tickets for my mum and dad to go to the evening performance. My mother once took me there to see a Shirley Temple film. I hated Shirley Temple and I made such a commotion that I had to be taken out.

Brian also went to the MIP to see *Gone with the Wind*, a classic he describes as 'a rather long drawn-out picture'. It was a summer evening and, at intermission time, the doors were opened and the audience all rushed outside to cool down. Randal Tighe often went to the MIP as a child and remembers that the film was always breaking down, and everybody jeered and stamped their feet. The MIP had been built in 1920, and replaced an earlier picture house, the Imperial Picture Palace, which had been on a different site. It lasted until 1959. Alban Leigh describes the beginning and end of the MIP:

I had always been told that my Uncle Henry had done a tap dance on stage the night the MIP opened. I was determined to be there on the picture house's last night, because I wanted to be last out when the MIP closed its doors for the last time.

The film Alban saw that night was a revival of the 1953 British film *The Cruel Sea*, starring Jack Hawkins. The building which was the MIP is still there, serving now as a market.

Moston is, perhaps, unique in having a picture house which began life as a tin hut, morphed into a picture palace and continues as a DIY warehouse/supplier. The Empress Picture Palace opened on Kenyon Lane in 1914, under the ownership of a Mr H. Senior. That building – the tin hut – was pulled down at the end of the 1930s and a new luxury cinema, the Adelphi, was built and opened in 1939. The site of the original picture house became a car park. The Adelphi was a purpose-built cinema. It didn't have a circle area, but the stalls seating sloped upwards and the seats at the rear of the stalls were tiered, and so more expensive. The main entrance, on Kenyon Lane, had glass display cases on either side. They contained stills of current pictures and

The Essoldo (formerly the
Rivoli), Collyhurst, 1957.
(Courtesy of Manchester
Archives and Local Studies,
Central Library)

Conran Street, Market
Harpurhey – former site of
the Princess Picture Hall.

Moston Imperial Palace,
now Moston Market.

adverts, and the adverts revolved. Patrons used the main entrance for the more expensive seats, but, to sit in the front stalls, you queued down the side of the picture house and went in near the screen. There was always a long queue on Kenyon Lane on a Saturday. Brian Lynch has this view of social status during the war years:

> I used to go to the Adelphi with my mum and dad. My mum would sometimes exclaim, 'Oh, look, there's Mrs … [our neighbour] sitting in the expensive seats.' On the rare occasions when we queued at the front entrance and went in the most expensive seats, Mum would make sure that we were noticed.

The Adelphi was part of the HDM circuit throughout its cinema life and lasted longer than many, finally closing in 1962 after a showing of the reissued double bill *Winchester 73* and *Sword of Ali Baba*. It reopened as a bingo hall; that too eventually closed. The building, quite obviously an old cinema, survives on Kenyon Lane, now housing the Deanway Home Centre.

Another Moston picture house opened the same year as the Adelphi. It was built at what was to be the junction of four roads, hence it was called the Fourways. When war broke out, the fourth way – Tindall Avenue – was never built, so the Fourways stood at the junction of only three roads. In the style of picture houses built in the 1930s, the Fourways was a large building, with 1,256 seats. Marjorie Thompson told me:

> I grew up not far from the Fourways. We had a farm (later demolished) behind our house, where Moss House School was built, and there were fields and a clay pit nearby. They have all gone now and the area is heavily built-up.

She also remembers that, when she went to the Fourways' Saturday matinees, the manager would stand at the front before the films started and blow a whistle. Everyone had to stand up and face the exits, in what she imagines must have been a fire drill. Programmes began each weekday at 2 p.m. and were continuous; you could stay in all day if you liked. The Fourways also showed films – usually old black-and-white movies – on a Sunday evening. Brian Lynch has a vivid memory of the Fourways:

> It was a nice picture house, very plush. There were two entrances: one at the front, one down the side. If you went in at the front entrance, you had to go through a foyer which was thickly carpeted and which had a shop and some fish tanks.

The Fourways survived the 1960s, and the decimation of picture houses in Manchester, finally ending its life in November 1973 when it was showing the ironically named James Bond picture *Live and Let Die*. It was eventually demolished and a block of flats were built on the site. Eddie Douglas, who lived in that area as a child, has an Aunty Pat, who worked at the Fourways as an usherette. Aunty Pat, Mrs Pat Rowe, started work at Moston Cotton Mill at the age of fifteen. Then, when she was seventeen, she also got a job at the Fourways. She remembers:

> I used to finish work at the mill at 5.30 p.m. and get the bus down Rochdale Road to the Fourways. The manager, Mr Atkinson, was a lovely man. I worked six nights and Saturday

The former Adelphi picture house, Moston 2009. Now the Deanway Home Centre.

afternoons, for £2 10s a week. We usherettes would be at the doors taking and tearing the tickets; we would put one half on a sharp stick and give the other half back to the customer. We had to show people to their seats, with a torch, when the film had started. We also sold ice cream in the intervals.

That was at the beginning of the 1950s, and Eddie, Aunty Pat's nephew who was a boy at the time, remembers:

Nana used to make some tea for Aunty Pat, because she didn't have time to come home between her two jobs. Then Nana would take me to the bus stop and see me onto the bus. I would ride the two stops to the Fourways to take Aunty Pat her tea. Sometimes she would let me stay in to see the picture.

Blackley was, in the pre-Greater Manchester years, the most northerly district of the city of Manchester. A picture house called the Victory, which had 1,367 seats, opened in 1923 on Charles Street (later Capstan Street). It quickly established itself as a very popular place for local people to have a night out, and it became a part of the HDM circuit. In 1940 the manager was Mr Sladen. On the night of 22 December 1940, Manchester was targeted by German bombers and the Blackley area was showered with incendiary bombs. Many fires were started, but local fire-fighters, aided by the ordinary people of Blackley, dealt very effectively with these. The *Middleton Guardian* reported, however:

The Fourways picture house, Moston. (Courtesy of Cinema Theatre Association, Tony Moss Collection)

An exception [to the slight damage caused] was a large cinema, where the roof was set alight. Before the fire could be got under control, the roof fell in and the flames roared skywards. Only the four walls were left standing.

The manager reported, 'There were no casualties, except the cat; she hasn't been seen since the bomb hit.' The Victory, for that was the 'large cinema' stricken, was to show *The Private Lives of Elizabeth and Essex*, starring Bette Davis as Queen Elizabeth I, the next day. It's not difficult to imagine Davis' Queen Elizabeth commanding, 'Get away from my picture house.' The Victory never reopened after the bombing. The four walls stood on the site for some twenty-six years until the site was cleared for a new school. Doreen Thompson thought the Victory was …

… a lovely place. The manager always wore evening dress. The seats at the front were benches. They used to make us move along the bench to get as many on as they could. The one on the end sometimes fell off.

Blackley's oldest picture house was on Factory Lane. Factory Lane is rather unusual, since one side of it is in Harpurhey and the other in Blackley. The picture house, the New Empire Electric Theatre, opened in 1913 on the Blackley side of the lane. The name was changed to Blackley Empire Electric Theatre; then it became Blackley Electric Theatre and finally, in 1939, the owners settled for the Empire Cinema. Janet McMullin lived on Factory Lane with her parents and sisters. Their house was just a few yards from the Empire and Janet used to go there with her sisters. Janet recalls:

CINEMA BURNED OUT

On Sunday evening a certain Manchester district was showered by incendiary bombs. The civilian population responded magnificently, men and women rushing into the streets, despite the danger, and tackling the hundreds of small fires which occurred. So well did they augment the work of the official fire-fighting services that the resulting damage was very slight. An exception was a large cinema, where the roof was set alight. Before it could be got under control the roof fell in, and the flames roared skywards.

Mr. Sladen, the manager, showed a "Guardian" reporter round the charred and blackened ruins. Only the four walls were left standing. "There were no casualties," said Mr. Sladen, "except the cat. She has not been seen since."

Water pressure was so low at the mains that hoses had to be laid to some public baths nearly a quarter of a mile away.

News report of the destruction of the Victory picture house, Blackley, by a bomb.

One day, my mum gave my oldest sister some money and told her to take me to the pictures. I was just four years old, but Mum told me to say I was five, if they asked me; otherwise they would not let me in. When we got to the pay box, the lady said, 'And how old are you, my love?'

'I'm four, but my mum says I have to say I'm five,' I answered. They would not let me in and my sister was furious because she had to take me back home.

Janet, and her sister, Maureen Hodson, both remember the children's matinees at the Empire on Saturday afternoons. There was a children's club, called the Roy Rogers' Club (Roy Rogers was a famous cowboy star, with a horse called Trigger). One Saturday the manager, Mr Wilkinson, organised a competition and asked all the children to dress as cowboys and cowgirls. Maureen worked as an usherette at the Empire when she left school.

It was a lovely place; there was no balcony, but the floor sloped up towards the back. You went to the more expensive seats through a very nice foyer. There was a side entrance for the cheaper seats. Mr Wilkinson was a lovely man. Each usherette had her own area, where she would show people to their seats. We also took it in turns to sell ice cream during the interval. We carried a tray of ice cream fastened around our necks. We walked backwards down the aisle in our high heels, and not one of us ever fell.

Janet McMullin – *née* Nish (front left) – her sister Stella, and two cousins outside their house. The Empire, Blackley, is in the background.

The Empire was a working cinema till Saturday, 12 March 1960. It closed that day after the last showing of *The Story of Dr Wassell*, a Gary Cooper film which had been made in 1943. The building was later demolished.

Maureen Hodson also went for a job as an usherette at another Blackley picture house, but the manager said she was not old enough. The Palladium stood on Rochdale Road, next to Beech Mount. The Blackley Palais de Danse had opened there in 1928; two years later it became the Palladium picture house. The building included a café and upstairs there was a ballroom. There was also a shopping arcade. The Palladium was a large hall, with seats for 1,750 people. When the picture house opened the manager was a Mr E. Anderton. Alban Leigh went to the Palladium in 1938, when he was six, to see Jeanette MacDonald and Allan Jones in the musical *The Firefly*. The score contained 'The Donkey serenade', which became Alban's favourite song. The Palladium, in a prime position on Rochdale Road, did good business into the 1950s. In 1954 it was renamed the Cintra, and its first film was *Dangerous Crossing*, starring Jeanne Crain. As the Cintra, however, it had a short life – a little over eight years. It ended its cinema days on Saturday, 19 May 1962, when it was showing reissues of Dean Martin and Jerry Lewis in *Hollywood or Bust*, and Burt Lancaster in *Gunfight at the OK Corral*. The building reopened as Cintra Bingo, and sisters Janet McMullin and Maureen Hodson both worked there. Cintra Bingo lasted for some forty years, until the building was closed and demolished in 2006.

Rochdale Road, passing through Blackley, is crossed by Victoria Avenue. The junction is a prime location and in 1932 a new cinema was built there, opening in August of that year. The Victoria Avenue Cinema had 1,400 seats on one floor, which sloped upwards from the stage towards the back, where the dearest seats were. The Victoria, dubbed the Vicky Avenue by locals, could also hold stage shows. To facilitate that, it had six dressing rooms. A week after it opened, the Four Saxon Girls gave dancing displays on stage.

The Victoria eventually became known as the Avenue and also became part of the ABC circuit, remaining so for the rest of its cinema life. Its prominent position at the junction and its easy accessibility helped keep it in business for forty years. It closed on 3 June 1972, when it was showing a cinema adaptation of the television comedy *Please Sir*. At the time of its closure

The Palladium/Cintra picture house, Blackley, 1957. (Courtesy of Manchester Archives and Local Studies, Central Library)

it was known simply as the ABC. It reopened, like so many others, for bingo, but closed finally in 1973. The building was not demolished until 1985. Syd Raynor, who has lived in Brisbane Australia since 1949, lived in Blackley when he was a boy. He has vivid memories of – and a personal involvement in – the Avenue:

> The building had two towers at the front corners. The towers were originally topped by amber-coloured glass domes. The domes were removed in 1939 (presumably with the outbreak of war) and lay gathering dust on the stage behind the screen. The manager, Billy Thornber, had been a variety entertainer – a comedian. He used to MC a short local talent show between the Avenue's two evening performances. Every evening he was in the foyer wearing a dinner jacket and black tie, greeting the patrons. The under-manager and the projectionist saw to the technical side of the picture house and the manageress and chief usherette looked after the in-house side of things.

Ken Martin recalls:

> The projectionist, called Eric, cosseted those projectors as if they were his children. He would spend hours cleaning and dusting them, wiping the lens, oiling the pulleys, slowly running the films through a separate machine to find any flaws or blemishes. That projection room, I swear, was cleaner than any hospital theatre.

Alban Leigh, aged five, with his mother. He heard 'The Donkey Serenade', which became his favourite song, at the Palladium Blackley.

Ken, twelve years old, used to sit in the projection room, idly going through a box full of glossy stills. Eric would say, 'Help yourself; take some home.' How Ken wishes he had – they would be worth a fortune now. Syd Raynor says:

Programmes changed on Thursdays; though, if a film was very popular, it was sometimes kept for a week. In 1939 seats cost 4d, if you entered via the bottom pay box down a side alley, and 6d or 9d if you entered via the main pay box. For Saturday matinees it was 2d anywhere. There were also Sunday shows, which were very popular. People would start queuing before 6 p.m. to be sure of being seated before the start at 6.30 p.m. – all to see two old pictures and a couple of cartoons. I had a job in the projection box for some time. I had to stand at the side of the projector and watch the film through the viewing window. It was all to do with very strict fire regulations. In those days film stock was nitrate and very flammable. All areas of the building where film was handled had to be separated from the public areas by fireproof barriers, including the small window between the projection box and the auditorium. My job was to watch the window. When I left Blackley for Australia in 1949, the Avenue was a thriving picture house. It had been owned by two brothers, Sam and Joe Haling, but Sam had died when I worked there. His ghost was supposed to haunt the landing midway up the stairs leading from the foyer to the projection box. Sam's ghost was blamed for any mishap, however slight or serious, which occurred during the running of a show.

The Avenue picture house, Blackley.

The interior of the Avenue picture house, Blackley.

NEWSREEL BOY

Ken Martin, seventy-seven years old this year, remembers his evening job:

In the grim days of 1944, at the age of twelve, like most lads I had a paper round – six mornings before school, six evenings after school, and Sunday mornings, come hail, rain, snow, fog, plague, chicken pox or measles. And my recompense for this? Three half crowns (about 40p in today's money). One Saturday afternoon, with jingling pennies and a bag of toffees in my pocket, I trudged off to the Avenue cinema for my weekly dose of film fun and derring do! I saw that many westerns, I was saddle sore. That Saturday, however, I was to embark on a whole new career. I handed over my 4*d* for a seat in the first fourteen rows for the afternoon kids' matinee. The ticket desk lady, a neighbour of my dear mother, asked me to go to the front of the house and report to Mr Eric Thornber, a dapper, be-suited gentleman, who was the manager of this opulent palace of glamorous entertainment. After a couple of probing questions about my availability, indeed my immediate availability for that very evening, and about my running prowess, Mr Thornber offered me the job of newsreel boy. The current boy had broken his leg. I would get 7*s* 6*d* a week, and free entrance to the Avenue on Sunday – my night off – when there was no newsreel. I was to report to Chief Projectionist Eric (chief projectionist? There was only one!) for my instructions. My job, I was told, would be to ferry the newsreel between the Avenue and the Palladium each evening. The two picture houses shared the newsreel. The work was organised like a military operation, meticulously timetabled to fit in with the Number 17 Rochdale-Manchester-Rochdale bus timetable. As soon as the newsreel end-title came up Bert would rewind the film, carefully put it in its container, and would bellow at me 'Run, lad, run!' He would add as an aside, 'Don't get knocked down, but, if you do, make sure the film can is all right.' He would thrust the can into my hands and I would literally race down the winding marble staircase into the palatial art-deco foyer. I would charge out of the glass front doors, hurried along by the scarlet-coated, gold-braided commissionaire, and dive headlong into the lurking Number 17 bus, often assisted by the clutching hands of the bus guard on my collar and britches! My life depended on the driver knowing I was 'on'. My two mile, one penny journey took eight minutes. Before I reached the portals of the Palladium I could hear the fretful projectionist, Fred, screaming, 'Come on, come on, Bobby; get your arse up here. We're late!' I can't imagine why he called me Bobby, but I lived with it. The patrons watching the newsreel in the two cinemas had no idea of how I took my life in my hands to ensure they got to see 'The news'.

FOUR

CHEETHAM AND CHEETHAM HILL

Cheetham Hill Road, one of the main arteries of Manchester, twists and turns its way north, through Cheetham and Cheetham Hill, until it becomes Bury New Road. The cinema page of the *Manchester Evening News* in the 1940s listed two Cheetham cinemas – the Temple and Odeon – and two in Cheetham Hill – the Premier and the Greenhill. Two others, not advertised in the newspaper, were also in Cheetham Hill – the Shakespeare and the Globe. The proliferation of picture houses in the area was probably due to the fact that it was a heavily-populated area, home of Manchester's Jewish community.

The Temple Pictorium opened in November 1913 with 846 seats and a prominent position on Cheetham Hill Road. Dorothy Cartledge, a child in Cheetham Hill during the Second World War, was forbidden to go to the Temple – as it quickly became known – because it was, to use her words, 'a bug hut'. Norah Walsh, who was familiar with all of the picture houses along Cheetham Hill Road as a girl, echoes Dorothy's opinion: 'it was a bit of a dump.' Trudy Philips lived as a child on North Street, just round the corner from the Temple. She went to Saturday morning children's matinees there, seeing cartoons, Superman serials, and Gene Autry and Roy Rogers' westerns. Her abiding memory, though, is of going with her older sister, an usherette at the Temple, to see Peter Cushing and Christopher Lee in *Dracula*, in the late 1950s. Trudy, who was scared stiff, has never been able to watch a horror film since. The Temple, a single-storey building, survived longest of the six Cheetham picture houses, lasting, rather surprisingly, into the 1980s. That was probably because the management was prepared to move with the times.

In the summer of 1972 the Temple closed for alterations, reopening on 21 August as the Temple Twins. The opening pictures were Walt Disney's *Sleeping Beauty* in Temple 1 and *Fiddler on the Roof* in Temple 2. Given a new lease of life, the Temple lasted for another eleven years after reopening, finally closing on 28 December 1983, when Temple 1 was showing *Krull* and Temple 2 *Sex in a Women's Prison*. The building was left to deteriorate for some years before it was finally demolished in the late 1990s.

A little further up Cheetham Hill Road, at its junction with Queen's Road, a new picture palace opened on 14 May 1931. The Riviera, which was to have been called the King George, could seat 2,117 people: 1,625 in the stalls and 492 in the balcony. Its prominent position and

Composite advert for the opening of the Riviera (later Odeon) in 1931, and for other cinemas in Cheetham and Cheetham Hill in the 1950s.

Temple picture house, Cheetham, in 1968. (Courtesy of Cinema Theatre Association archive)

Odeon, Cheetham, in 1959, showing the John Mills/Hayley Mills film *Tiger Bay*. (Courtesy of Manchester Archives and Local Studies, Central Library)

Cover of the souvenir programme for the opening of the Premier picture house, Cheetham Hill, 1925.

hint of luxury ensured the Riviera very quickly became a favourite venue for a nice night out. Dorothy Cartledge remembers:

> The Riviera was a lovely comfortable place. We used to go there to watch cowboy pictures at children's matinees. I remember going there when I was nine, with a boyfriend – well, a friend who was a boy – and taking chopped-up carrots to munch, because we couldn't afford sweets, which were rationed anyway.

J. Arthur Rank, who would become the most important cinema proprietor in the UK, took one look at the Riviera and decided he wanted it in his cinema collection. He took the Riviera over in 1938. In 1943 it was renamed the Odeon, and so it stayed for the rest of its picture house life. Norah Walsh recalls visiting the Odeon:

> The Odeon was the *crème de la crème* of picture houses. It was very clean and bright. It had smartly dressed usherettes, who actually showed you to your seat. I went there a lot as a child to the Saturday morning children's shows, usually to see Roy Rogers and his horse Trigger. There always used to be a sing-song, the words being projected onto the screen and a bouncing ball pointing out the syllables. There were also competitions; I remember one to see how many times you could write your name on the back of a postage stamp – a bit unfair if your writing was large! I went to the Odeon with my then boyfriend to see one of my favourite pictures, John Ford's western *She Wore a Yellow Ribbon*.

At the beginning of the 1960s the Rank Organisation decided to rationalise its cinema circuit, and the axe fell on many Odeon cinemas. The Odeon at Cheetham Hill fell victim to the cull, closing on 4 March 1961. Its last film was Kenneth More's comedy *Man in the Moon*, supported by *Marriage of Convenience*. The building reopened as a Top Rank Bowl(ing alley), which eventually closed. The building was demolished and a huge shopping complex, the Manchester Fort, now occupies the site.

A couple of miles up Cheetham Hill Road, on the opposite side, the New Premier picture house opened on 3 August 1925. This large hall, seating almost 2,000 people, was owned by Circuit Cinemas Ltd. Within four years, however, as sound was making an impression in films, the New Premier was taken over by ABC and stayed with them for the remainder of its life as a picture house. ABC renamed it the ABC Premier in 1929. Arthur Back, who often went to the picture house, remembers it being very posh: 'There were double seats for courting couples in the back rows. I was a member of the ABC Minors' Club, and used to go on Saturday mornings. The last film I ever saw at the Premier was *Zulu*.'

The Premier occupied a good site on Cheetham Hill Road. There were two rival picture houses within yards, but it was an up-market place which people loved to visit. Norah Walsh remembers that her parents only took her to the Premier when they could afford it, because the seats were more expensive than in the other cinemas. She loved the Edgar Lustgarten Scotland Yard mysteries (supporting films that ran about an hour) and, although she had a boyfriend who took her there to see every western that ever played the cinema, she preferred the Hollywood

Interior of the New Premier, later ABC Premier picture house, Cheeham Hill.

musicals. Her favourite was *Three Little Words*, MGM's Technicolor story of songwriters Bert Kalmar and Harry Ruby, which distorted the facts but had stunning guest stars.

The Premier, which ended up simply as the ABC, kept going until 1970. On Saturday 25 July, after the final showing of *Kes*, supported by *The Thousand Plane Raid*, the picture house closed. It later became a snooker hall and, when that too eventually closed, the building was demolished.

Halliwell Lane joins Cheetham Hill Road just a few yards above where the Premier stood. A picture house called the Shakespeare Picture Palace opened on Halliwell Lane in January 1914 and had a life span of some forty-five years. Norah Walsh remembers it as 'not a very nice place'. But that didn't stop her begging her parents to take her there to see the technicolored pirate epic *The Spanish Main* in 1945. Norah also has vivid memories of seeing *How Green Was My Valley* at the Shakespeare and 'crying and crying'. The Shakespeare, as it was popularly known, did good business in the boom years of cinema. Arthur Back remembers going to children's matinees there, and his mum taking him and his sister to evening shows: 'The Shakespeare was a moderate size, but a bit run down. My mum used to take us there, and always took a packet of sandwiches for us to eat in the interval.'

With the increasing ownership of televisions in the 1950s, and the close proximity of two other picture houses, the Shakespeare began to struggle for paying customers. Its owners saw its salvation in a change of emphasis, closing the Shakespeare on 20 January 1956 and reopening it three days later as the Continental. Its big selling point was that it showed classy European films and was 'only ten minutes from town'. It certainly reopened with a prestige picture, Federico Fellini's *La Strada*. Unfortunately it was in the wrong place for an art house cinema, and there was already a city centre venue showing new European movies. The Continental was quickly reduced to showing suggestively titled and X certificated European sex movies or horror/fantasy pictures. It closed just a week before its first birthday as the Continental, when it was showing the monster movie *Rodan*. The building was eventually demolished and Cheetham Hill's first supermarket was built on the site.

The Premier was not the first picture house in Cheetham Hill to bear that name. Stand today at the corner of Cheetham Hill Road and Waterloo Road, and you will see, almost directly opposite, the stalls of fruit and vegetables of a greengrocer's spilling out onto the pavement.

Back row: Jessie Ismay, Harry Howell and Beatrice Howell; front row: Norman Howell. Jessie and Beatrice were usherettes at the Premier, Harry was projectionist there.

The Greenhill picture house, Cheetham Hill, *c.* 1937.

The building in which the business is housed opened in 1920 as the Premier Picture Hall. In 1925 the proprietors, Circuit Cinemas Ltd (the cinema was later taken over by Union Cinemas), built a new luxury picture house across the road; they gave that one the name Premier, and renamed the original Premier the Greenhill – a name it kept till it closed – perhaps because Greenhill Road is nearby. Dorothy Cartledge remembers, 'It wasn't a very nice picture house and my parents wouldn't allow me to go there.' But Norah Walsh remembers the Greenhill as 'a brighter, cleaner place than some'.

The Greenhill's good position, on a major bus route to Manchester, kept it in business for more than forty years, despite the close proximity of the Premier and the Shakespeare. Its demise came on Saturday, 19 May 1962, after the last showing of *The Guns of Navarone*. The building did reopen, like so many, for bingo, and survives today – one of the few surviving picture house buildings – albeit now the premises of a greengrocer.

The last and, it seems, least of Cheetham Hill's six picture houses was opened in 1912 on Thomas Street, which runs alongside the cemetery. The Globe was a modest size, seating 750 patrons, but it was, says Arthur Back, 'a bug hut. The front rows were not seats but wooden benches.' Myrna Marks, who lived in the area as a child, remembers that her dad used to take her to the Greenhill, the Premier, the Shakespeare, the Riviera and the Globe. She too remembers the Globe as a bug hut: 'It had a corrugated iron roof, and was very noisy when it rained.' The Globe, which belonged for some time to the HDM circuit, generally showed pictures which had played at another Cheetham Hill house months earlier. In spite of this, it continued in business longer than one would have expected, perhaps because it was in a built-up area and some distance away from the other Cheetham Hill picture houses. It finally closed its doors in 1957 and has since been pulled down.

FIVE

CHORLTON-ON-MEDLOCK, HULME, MOSS SIDE AND FALLOWFIELD

Oxford Street turns into Oxford Road, passing beneath the Mancunian Way flyover, into the district of Chorlton-on-Medlock, the home of Manchester University. For fifty years or so the district was also home to four picture houses, all of which flourished, despite their closeness to the city centre houses of Oxford Street.

Nearest to the city was the Grosvenor, opened in May 1915 by the Lord Mayor of Manchester, on the corner of Grosvenor Street and Oxford Road. The opening film was *Jane Shore*, advertised as 'The world's masterpiece in five acts and two hundred and fifty scenes'. The new picture house had 1,000 seats priced at 6*d* or 1*s* and ran continuous performances from 2.30 p.m. to 10.30 p.m. It quickly became a popular venue for a night out and, even when the Gaumont and Paramount – two luxury picture palaces – opened less than half a mile away on Oxford Street, and had first choice of the new pictures, the Grosvenor flourished, eventually as part of the HDM circuit. The picture business in the 1950s was cut-throat though, and the Grosvenor management was not always quick to grasp new opportunities. When Twentieth Century Fox introduced CinemaScope with *The Robe* in the winter of 1953, most picture houses jumped on the bandwagon very quickly. The Grosvenor, however, did not install a CinemaScope screen until the winter of 1955. The Grosvenor was eventually sold to the Star circuit in the early 1960s, joining the Regal Twins a hundred or so yards away across Oxford Road. Those were parlous times for old-style picture houses and the Grosvenor was eventually forced to rely on a diet of sex/horror pictures for part of the week and bingo for the rest. Roy Pennill remembers the Grosvenor as:

> ... lacking in atmosphere, and this detracted from my enjoyment of the film. The auditorium was as miserable as the green and cream tiled façade and the non-inviting foyer. I have never met anyone who regarded the Grosvenor as their regular cinema.

The Grosvenor's days as a picture house finally ended on Saturday, 18 May 1968, when it was showing a double bill of *Passionate Demons* and *Attack of the Crab Monsters*. The building

Composite advert for picture houses in Chorlton-on-Medlock, Hulme and Moss Side, and the opening of the refurbished Plaza, Oxford Road.

became a full-time bingo hall and still stands on the corner of Grosvenor Street, looking very dilapidated, now a pub called the Footage and Firkin.

For four years after it opened the Grosvenor had no closer competitor than the New Oxford, which was in the city on Oxford Street. In 1919, however, a new picture house, fancifully named La Scala, opened just 100 yards away, on the corner of Booth Street East and Oxford Road. The owner was Mr B. Rhodes, and it was not just a picture house, with more than 2,000 seats, but also a ballroom and café. The original entrance was on Booth Street East, but the owner, quickly realising that an entrance on Oxford Road would bring in more paying customers, took over three shops to provide such an entrance.

There was room for two picture houses in that densely-populated part of the city and the Grosvenor and La Scala both flourished through the 1920s. La Scala was adapted for the new talking pictures in September 1929, when it showed its first talkie, strangely entitled *The Dummy*. In March 1935 it became part of the ABC circuit, with access to all the ABC releases. It remained ABC until August 1945, when it closed for some weeks. It reopened with new owners: the Granada circuit, and a new name: the Roxy. Granada retained it until the late 1940s, when they sold it to John Buckley. In the early 1950s, with innovations like 3D and CinemaScope, the picture business flourished, but television was a massive threat. John Buckley, well aware of this, decided on an audacious move to give his Manchester picture house a new lease of life and make it one of the leading picture houses in the city. He closed the Roxy in January 1958. When it reopened, it had been completely refurbished and had a new name, the Plaza.

Moreover, as Mr T. Poole remembers, 'The Plaza had a real biggie for its opening. The Cecil B. De Mille picture *The Ten Commandments* was the Plaza's opening film, and Charlton Heston, who starred as Moses, was in attendance at the opening performance.'

The De Mille epic, in VistaVision and Technicolor and with a starry cast, had only opened in London's West End three months earlier, and it was a great coup for John Buckley to get its northern premiere for the Plaza. It would have been expected to open at the Odeon or Gaumont on Oxford Street. The film ran for more than five months at the Plaza, but proved to be a one-off success. The cinema was afterwards restricted to second-run films, which had played the Rank and ABC cinemas, and it existed on a diet of minor horror pictures and sex films. The end finally came in July 1965, when the Plaza was showing a double bill of a minor Italian picture *38 24 36* (Italian title *Canzoni Nel Mondo*) and *How I lived as Eve*. The Plaza closed

The Footage and Firkin public house, Oxford Road – formerly the Grosvenor picture house, Chorlton-on-Medlock.

The Roxy picture house, Oxford Road, shortly before it was closed, refurbished and reopened as the Plaza in 1956. (Courtesy of Manchester Archives and Local Studies, Central Library)

The former Rivoli, Denmark Road in 2009; now part of Manchester University.

after the final performance of those obscure pictures, remaining empty for five years before it was finally demolished in 1970.

Chorlton-on-Medlock's third, and oldest, picture house was much further out of town than the Grosvenor and La Scala. The Rivoli was on Denmark Street, alongside the Whitworth Art Gallery, with its entrance on Aberdeen Street. Opened in 1914, it was advertised in the *Manchester Evening News* with the Rusholme picture houses, in spite of its Chorlton-on-Medlock location. It had 1,100 seats, a stage and three dressing rooms, so it could hold stage performances. The location, close to the university with its hundreds of students, ensured the Rivoli soon became a popular venue. For a brief period in the 1920s it became a dance hall, reverting to being a picture house in 1929, probably with the coming of the talkies. Tony Clarke lived roughly three minutes' walk away from the Rivoli in the 1940s and 1950s:

My dad was boiler man there, my mum was a cleaner and my sister was the ice cream girl. I always got complimentary tickets, but unfortunately no complimentary ice cream! There was an old lady who sat just inside the entrance. You gave her your ticket and she tore it in two, gave half back to you and threaded the stub on a needle and thread. The Rivoli's foyer had a lovely carpet and polished brass and was always full of adverts for forthcoming attractions. Like most picture houses in those days it was always full, and, when they showed a reissue of *The Song of Bernadette*, there were queues around the building because so many Irish Catholic families lived in the area.

Not everyone agrees with Tony's recollections. Roy Clark recalls:

The Rivoli was a bit sleazy. It was always full, and it always smelled of San-Izal disinfectant. During the war it was frequented by American soldiers, and the supply of sweets, chocolate and chewing gum they gave us youngsters made our trips to the Rivoli all the more enjoyable.

The Rivoli survived as a picture house until the early 1960s when, in common with much of the area, it was among properties transferred to Manchester University, closing on 5 March 1960, after the final showing of *Pork Chop Hill* and *Crash Drive*. The building, just four years short of its centenary, remains on Denmark Street in 2010, and is now used to house the department which looks after the university's grounds.

The first Chorlton-on-Medlock picture house to open was the College Cinema, which opened in 1914 on Coupland Street, in the heart of the university area, where the hundreds of students ensured good attendances. It could seat 1,000 patrons, and seats were very modestly priced; as a result, it flourished for more than forty years, surviving until 1960. It closed on 13 February of that year, its final programme being *Blind Date* and *Tarawa Beachhead*. The building reopened as the College Theatre Club, and later became the Ardri Irish Club, but has now been demolished.

In recent years, despite Manchester City Council's efforts at regeneration, the Hulme area, south of the city, has been notorious ever since the botched rebuilding in the 1960s. In the first half of the twentieth century, as a result of an influx of people to meet increasing industrial demands, Hulme was densely populated. With the coming of moving pictures, Hulme had the capacity to provide constant large audiences, and, when picture-going was at its height in the

1940s, Hulme could boast no fewer than six picture houses. In 1911 the Bijou Electric Theatre opened on Erskine Street. It was a modestly sized house and prospered, becoming the Bijou New Cinema in the 1930s. In that same decade, however, the Bijou was demolished and a new picture house replaced it. The newcomer, the Luxor, opened on the site in 1938.

Dot Curzon, who was born at 88 Erskine Street in 1949, says: 'We lived next door but one to the Luxor picture house. We used to go on Saturday afternoons when they showed Hopalong Cassidy westerns, Flash Gordon serials and Little Rascal comedies. I remember the seats were very old.' John Briggs thought the Luxor 'a classy, well-kept place'. Seat prices were modest, kids paying 6d in the 1930s. Philip Johnston tells me, 'We used to hand over 6d and make our way to the cheapest seats. Then, at the first opportunity, we went to the toilet and sneaked back into the dearest seats.' The Luxor's life as a picture house lasted until the late 1950s, and it closed on 20 June 1959, after the final showing of *I Only Arsked* [*sic*] and *Buchanan Rides Alone*. It was revived later as a social club, the Luxor Club, which also eventually closed and was pulled down.

Chapman Street in Hulme, which changed to Cossack Street, is long gone now – swept away in the 1960s' regeneration. The street was once home to two picture houses. The Chapman Street Picture Palace first opened its doors in 1912, later changing its name to the Crescent. It was a fairly large house with room for 1,200 people. Cyril Walker, as a boy in the 1930s, used to go to the Crescent often. He recalls that, 'the fireman in the Crescent used to walk around with a spray, disinfecting the urchins,' and John Bridges, who also frequented the Crescent, remembers it as 'a purpose-built picture house, with a balcony; it was very well kept.' The people of the area kept the Crescent in business for nearly half a century, though things became increasingly difficult for its owners as the 1960s came in. The Crescent finally closed its doors on 5 June 1965, after the final showing of *Slave Merchants* and *Winnetou the Warrior*. When the council put its redevelopment plans into effect, Cossack (Chapman) Street vanished, along with the Crescent picture house.

When the Chapman Street Picture Palace opened in 1912, across the street, just a few yards away, was the Chapman Street Hall – a chapel. A few years later that small building, with seating for only 400 people, became the New Popular Picture House. John Briggs remembers it as 'rather drab and narrow, with a balcony that went round the two sides and the back of the building.' Picture-going was so popular among the working classes when John was a boy, in the 1940s, that there were queues six nights a week for the Crescent and the New Popular, which the locals called 'The Pop'. He only lived 100 yards away from both cinemas.

Alan Butler remembers the New Popular as 'a bug hut'. He recalls helping a friend of his, who was the projectionist at the New Popular, and says that one night the two of them nearly set the place on fire. Bug hut or not, the New Popular kept going into the 1960s, until, on Saturday, 7 January 1961, it finally closed its doors. The last films shown there were two minor pictures, *Follow that Horse* (a British farce) and *Dust in the Sun* (an Australian 'western'), the kind of programme which, perhaps, brought it to its knees. After its closure, the New Popular, along with its neighbour the Crescent and the whole of Cossack Street, vanished in the Hulme regeneration.

'Bug hut' and 'flea pit' are terms often used by older cinema-goers, not just in Manchester but in the author's birthplace in South Wales and, indeed, all over the country, to describe many of the myriad picture houses which flourished from the 1930s to the 1960s. People accustomed to modern multiplex cinemas would have no idea what the terms mean.

Bijou Theatre, Hulme, later the Luxor picture house. (Courtesy of Cinema Theatre Association archive)

Crescent picture house, Hulme, 1962. (Courtesy of Manchester Archives and Local Studies, Central Library)

Radnor picture house, Hulme, 1937. Destroyed by a German bomb in December 1940. (Courtesy of Manchester Archives and Local Studies, Central Library)

The New Popular was one of those described in this way in Hulme, but John Briggs knew another. He describes it thus:

> It was a tin hut with a corrugated iron roof. Whenever it rained heavily, you wouldn't believe how loud the noise inside the picture house was. If you were lucky enough to meet a girl, you'd be sure to take her to a better venue if she agreed to a date.

John was talking about the Lyceum, which opened on City Road, next to Malvern Street, around 1913. Bug hut it may have been, but it managed to stay in the business of showing pictures for forty-six years, for some of its life part of the J.T. Emery circuit. It closed on 12 December 1959, the last films shown being the obscure *Girls in Action* and *Down Beat*. The building was used as an Irish social club for some years after its closure, but was later demolished.

Of the two remaining picture houses in Hulme, one was – tragically – the shortest lived, the other, by contrast, the longest lasting. The Radnor opened on Radnor Street in 1937, under the ownership of Arthur Murray. Built on the site of the demolished Radnor Street Methodist Church, the Radnor was a purpose-built, luxury picture house, equipped with a stage and two dressing rooms, so that it could hold variety shows also. It could seat 1,100 people, with seats priced at 6d and 1s. Shows were continuous on weekdays, and there were two separate shows on a Saturday.

Cyril Walker, just nine years of age at the time, was at the opening of the Radnor, which was performed by comedian/ukulele player/film star George Formby. Cyril remembers having to climb up a lamp post to see George Formby. In heavily-populated Hulme, where the other cinemas had all been around for some years, the Radnor quickly became a very popular place for a night out – Hulme's favourite picture house – but it was to have a very short life. The Germans bombed Manchester in December 1940, and the Radnor was one of the buildings hit. Fortunately it was in the middle of the night, so there was no audience, but the picture house suffered so much internal damage that it was never able to reopen. The shell of the building remained on Radnor Street for many years before it was finally pulled down.

Hulme's longest lasting picture house began its life in 1928, on the site of the demolished Baptist Meeting House on York Street. Appropriately it was called the York. Owned by Thomas and Norman Royle, it could seat 1,400 people. John Briggs remembers it as 'a nice place. When I was a lad, one of our gang would pay to go in. Then he would go to the toilet and open a window, so the rest of us could get in through the window, free of charge.'

The York did good business for some thirty years, but, like many other local picture houses, found things difficult in the 1960s. The management finally decided to close it on 11 June 1966, when the programme was *Pirates of Blood River* and *Mysterious Island*. The building reopened as a bingo club, but that closed after two years. A Burnley company, Unit 4 Cinemas, then took over the building. Realising that large single-screen cinemas were no longer viable, the new owners converted the York to a multi-screen house, Unit 4. Screen 1, with 210 seats, was in the former circle area, and Screen 2 (101 seats), Screen 3 (102 seats) and Screen 4 (102 seats) were side-by-side in what had been the stalls area. They operated the complex for a few years, but in 1974, under new owners, it was renamed the Aaben, and programmed with films that appealed to the students and young professional people living in the area.

The derelict Aaben cinema, Hulme, formerly the York picture house, in the early 1990s; now demolished. (Courtesy of exHulme.co.uk)

The Aaben showed films from all over the world, especially Europe, as well as British and Hollywood pictures which were considered difficult to place by their producers. This author spent many happy hours in one or other of the Aaben's four screens during the 1970s and 1980s, retaining a vivid memory of seeing *The Creature from the Black Lagoon* there, in its original 3D form.

The four-screen picture house continued, under different owners, until the last decade of the twentieth century. By 1991 two of the screens had closed and the place was known as the Cinetheque. In that year it finally closed, and the building was left to become derelict and vandalised. When Manchester City Council decided to regenerate Hulme in 1993, the old picture house, which had gone through so many changes, was pulled down and replaced by new housing. Jeff McKenzie was a boy in the cinema's days as the Aaben:

> We used to do car-minding for people who went to the Aaben. When they drove into the car park at the rear of the building, we'd ask, 'Can I mind your car, please, mister?' They would give us 10 pence and we'd rush off to buy some sweets. The first film I saw at the Aaben was *Grease*, and it seemed like all the kids in Hulme were in there.

Hulme's neighbour, Moss Side, part of the city of Manchester since 1904, was originally a village with scarcely 200 inhabitants. The area saw a great influx of people looking for work during the Industrial Revolution, and thousands of cramped and unhygienic dwellings were

The Claremont picture house, Moss Side. (Courtesy of Cinema Theatre Association archive)

built to house them. Today, heavily-populated Moss Side struggles with its reputation for gangs, drugs and drive-by killings – while there's not a picture house to be seen.

There were originally two – or, some would say, three – picture houses in Moss Side. The first, the Princess picture house, opened in 1913 on Raby Street, between Westwood Street and Moss Lane East. The Princess was small, with seating for 540 people, and it was originally owned by a man named Bernard Knowles. As in most local picture houses, seats were modestly priced, at 4d and 9d, and there were two shows nightly. The Princess, next to the Temperance Billiard Hall, survived into the 1930s; it closed down in 1938 and has since been demolished.

Princess Road and Wilmslow Road run parallel through Moss Side. They are connected by Upper Lloyd Street. On 1 February 1923, a new picture house opened on the corner of Upper Lloyd Street and Claremont Road. A purpose-built house, seating some 1,700 people, the Claremont Super Cinema had weekday evening programmes continuous from 5.30 p.m., with a matinee every day. On Saturday there were continuous performances from 2.30 p.m. A good location, and the absence of any close competition, ensured the Claremont's success. This did not go unnoticed, soon attracting the attention of the fledgling ABC circuit; in 1929 it became part of that organisation, staying with ABC for almost thirty years. Brian Philbrock was a six-year-old when his dad died and his mum was left to bring up Brian and his sister alone. Brian says:

We lived in Moss Side and my mother got a job as an usherette at the Claremont every afternoon and evening. I used to go to the Claremont three times a week, once to see the Monday/Tuesday/Wednesday show, once to see the Thursday/Friday/Saturday show and once on Saturday morning to the children's matinee. The picture house had a gold/orange interior, with lights in the shape of fiery torches around the walls. The Claremont had a circle and a grand staircase leading up to it. Because my mother worked there I could get in for half price – 3d in the stalls, 6d in the circle; I also got ice cream half price. On Saturday morning

Edna and Cyril Philbrock, 1929.
Edna worked as an usherette at the
Claremont, Moss Side.

at the children's show there would be competitions. An expert would demonstrate the yo-yo and then the kids would try. Another competition was called Hi-Lo. The kids would have a bat with a small ball attached to it by elastic. The winner would be the youngster who could bat the ball longest and in the most skilful way.

Jo Hayes, a girl in Moss Side in the early 1950s, says:

> My sister had a boyfriend and she would go to the Claremont with him because he lived near there. I used to follow them and sit behind them. My sister was always telling me to go away, and sit somewhere else, but I never would until she bribed me.

ABC finally decided to close the picture house in 1958, and the last film shown there, on Saturday 8 February, was *Robbery Under Arms* starring Peter Finch. The building survived for another sixteen years, finally being demolished in 1974. John Briggs, a boy in the 1940s, remembers visiting the Claremont on Sunday nights: 'There was only one show on Sundays, usually two old black-and-white films. I remember that the Claremont had a commissionaire, a little fellow, who kept the kids in order.'

Moss Side and Fallowfield are adjoining districts of Manchester. The Royal Electric Theatre opened on the corner of Princess Road and Moss Lane East in 1915. It was a large hall, seating more than 1,500 people, and its good position on a main road ensured its initial success. As cinema-going increased, with the coming of the talkies in the late 1920s, the Royal Electric Theatre changed its name to the Capitol. Alan Butler knew the picture house as the Capitol and he recalls:

> I used to go there on Saturday mornings with my mates to see serials like *The Crawling Hand*. It was something of a bug hut. Sometimes, if we were short of money, one of the lads would buy a ticket and go in. Then he would open a fire door and let the rest of us in.

Brian Philbrock remembers being in the Capitol one Saturday for the children's matinee when the screen caught fire:

> A black mark appeared in the centre of the screen and spread outwards and the whole cinema was very quickly filled with smoke. There was no panic. They got us all out very quickly. I went home, but had to wait outside the house until my mum returned from doing the shopping.

The Capitol continued to do good business and, in 1948, another name change occurred. In January of that year, *Manchester Evening News* adverts said that the Capitol was to become the Wycliffe. The Wycliffe did well – like most picture houses at the end of the 1940s and in the early years of the 1950s. Then, again like many of its fellows, it began to find audiences harder to entice. It struggled on until 1968, on a programme of reissues of old pictures and, as John Briggs remembers, looking 'grubby and uncared for'. The axe finally fell on Saturday, 7 September 1968, when the picture house was showing a double bill of *The Ballad of Josie*, starring Doris Day, and *Shenandoah*, a James Stewart western. The building reopened for bingo and, when that ended, it remained on Princess Road – shabby and increasingly derelict – until it was finally demolished in 1990, since which time the site has been vacant.

The term 'bug hut', frequently used for some picture houses, had existed for some years. Jean Dunn knew the Capitol/Wycliffe and tells this apocryphal story on the subject of 'bug huts':

> My mother, Doris Smales, held down two jobs in the 1930s. After finishing her day job, she worked as an usherette at the Capitol in Moss Side. She first had to serve as cashier in the pay box; then she would put on a lace apron and headdress and sell ice cream. That done, she was allowed to watch the rest of the film. In the flashes of light from the screen, you could see the mice and beetles running around. People would have put their coats on the seats; they would dangle on the floor, so they would take some unwanted company home with them.

Doris Smales-Grandthorne, who also worked as an usherette at the Claremont.

The Wycliffe cinema, looking badly run down in 1967. It lasted another year before closure. (Courtesy of Manchester Archives and Local Studies, Central Library)

The Cresta (formerly Regent) picture house, Moss Side, in 1959. (Courtesy of Manchester Archives and Local Studies, Central Library)

Early in its life, the Royal Electric Theatre was advertised as being in Fallowfield. As it became the Capitol, then the Wycliffe, the *Manchester Evening News* included it among the Moss Side picture houses. People brought up in the area will have their own opinions about which is correct.

A late arrival on the scene, opening in 1929, was the Regent on Princess Road South. Purpose-built, and designed for stage performances, it also had six dressing rooms, seating for 1,300 customers, continuous performances daily and prices from 8*d* to 1*s* 6*d*. Its comparatively luxurious ambience – no bug hut this – made the Regent a runaway success. Mavis Ward lived near the Regent when she was a girl. In fact, she and the cinema were born in the same year – Mavis in July, the Regent in August. She recalls:

> As a little girl, I used to go to the Regent with my mother and father. We always sat near the left-hand side because there was room for Dad to stretch his legs out. In the interval between the pictures, a lady dressed all in black played the piano on stage.

John Briggs, too, knew the Regent as a boy. He remembers:

> You didn't get a ticket, but a metal disc, which you handed to the usherette. When she had collected quite a few, she returned them to the pay box lady, who slipped them, one by one, onto a metal holder, to be used for later customers. It was a very noisy process, which could be heard wherever you sat in the place.

In its early days and into the 1950s, the Regent was advertised, along with the Capitol (Wycliffe) and Claremont, as being in Moss Side. The Regent had a ticket office at the front of the cinema, on Stockport Road. At the side there was a kind of covered way which led to the back and another ticket office. If you went in that way you entered the building near the screen. Jo Hayes used to go to the Capitol when she was a girl in the early 1950s:

> We used to play in the covered way at the side. The place had a commissionaire, a very big man whom we affectionately called 'Fat Fred'. He was always trying to chase us out but could never catch us. He used to go round during the performance with a torch. If he saw anyone up to mischief, he would say, 'I'll chuck you out'. But he never did. He was a really nice man.

In 1954 the Regent's name was changed to the Cresta. At that point it began to be advertised as being in Fallowfield, and so it remained for the rest of its life – which was not a long one. It closed on 30 April 1960, after the final showing of *Tommy the Toreador*, a Technicolor musical starring pop-star Tommy Steele. A petrol station now occupies the site.

SIX

LONGSIGHT AND LEVENSHULME

Longsight and Levenshulme lie on either side of Stockport Road as it winds its way from Ardwick Green to Stockport. These two districts could boast no fewer than eight picture houses between them – two of them picture palaces to rival those in centre of Manchester.

Between Kirkmanshulme Lane and Stanley Grove, two of Longsight's picture houses faced each other across Stockport Road. The King's – originally the King's Opera House – opened in October 1905, the proprietor being W.J. Broadhead, who owned other theatres in the Manchester area. Brian Gregson, a boy in Longsight in the 1930s, remembers seeing the name 'The King's Opera House' in coloured glass on the outside of the theatre. The King's operated as a theatre for many years. Dorothy Barron, who lived in Longsight as a girl, remembers her mother telling her that a very young Charlie Chaplin once appeared at the King's with Fred Karno's company. Her mother used to say, when chaos reigned at home, 'It's like Karno's circus!'

When sound was firmly established in film in the early 1930s, a decision was taken to turn the King's into a cinema. Consequently, in 1932, the building was sold to H.D. Moorhouse and became part of the HDM circuit. Stage performances ceased within a year. Christine Boyall, who visited the King's in the 1940s, says:

> I don't think it had changed much from the theatre. There were still boxes along the sides. The main entrance was on Stockport Road, but there was also an entrance on a side street. I used to go there with my mum or with my school friends.

As a picture house the King's had a Saturday afternoon children's matinee. Walter Pennington grew up in Longsight and went to those matinees in the 1930s:

> I well remember going to the pictures as a lad in the 1930s, every Saturday afternoon. Almost next to the King's was a large greengrocer's called Allendales. On Saturdays we would queue up to buy a penny bag of peanuts. A good proportion was just thrown around. The staff must have taken ages to clean up for the evening performance.

King's Opera House, which became King's Cinema, Longsight.

Two decades later, Graham Todd grew up in Longsight. He remembers the Longsight picture houses when they were on their last legs:

> The King's was the most popular of the three. But it used to draw an unsavoury element, perhaps kids from the notorious Chell Street area behind the cinema. They were very unruly, always chucking things down from the balcony or spitting on the unwary ones below in the stalls. Once someone brought an air pistol and fired at the cowboys on the screen. The screen was perforated and had to be replaced or stitched together. After that there was always a compulsory gun check at the ticket desk.

The King's, increasingly dilapidated, continued until 1964. The building remained for some time until it was destroyed by fire. Graham Todd was there:

> I recall vividly the demise of the King's, which went up in flames. I was there to see all the fire engines on Stockport Road. The King's died magnificently, with the roof, well ablaze, collapsing amid the sound of crackling flames and breaking timbers. We were so close you could feel the heat scorching your skin.

Almost directly opposite the King's was the Shaftesbury, opened in 1913 by the Shaftesbury Cinema Theatre Company. While the King's had seating for more than 1,100 people, the Shaftesbury could almost match it, with 1,050 seats. Together the two picture houses dominated the stretch of Stockport Road between Kirkmanshulme Lane and Dickinson Road for half a century. In the 1940s the Shaftesbury joined the King's as part of the HDM circuit. Elsie Swainson lived in Chorlton-on-Medlock as a child and was familiar with the Longsight picture houses. She recalls:

> Most of the children in Chorlton-on-Medlock went to the Saturday afternoon shows at the King's or the Shaftesbury. We always walked there and back. Two pence admission bought a short picture, a cartoon, an episode of a serial and a travel film, plus a short RKO news. The King's and the Shaftesbury had almost the same programme, except for the serial. So, if you fancied a cowboy film with Tom Mix, or a comedy with Charlie Chaplin, you could change cinemas from week to week.

The Shaftesbury, like the King's, soldiered on until Saturday, 27 May 1961 when it closed. The last film shown there was the Disney film *The Big Fisherman*, starring, as Simon Peter, musical star Howard Keel, who didn't sing a note in it. The Shaftesbury building was later demolished to make way for shops. Walter Pennington, like Elsie Swainson, remembers the Saturday matinees, but slightly differently:

> Perhaps because the two picture houses belonged to the HDM circuit, they showed the same serial – Flash Gordon, Buck Rogers, Hopalong Cassidy. But one of the picture houses was always a week ahead of the other, so, if you missed an episode of the serial in one, you could catch up with it at the other the next week.

Further along Stockport Road, just before its junction with Slade Lane, a new picture house opened in 1914. The Queen's Picture Theatre was an imposing addition to Stockport Road, with its tiered and arched frontage and its name on the top of the tower over the entrance.

Jack Reynolds, projectionist at the Shaftesbury picture house, Longsight.

The Queen's picture house, Longsight, 1958. (Courtesy of Manchester Archives and Local Studies, Central Library)

The Queen's, like most local picture houses in the 1940s and 1950s, changed its programme midweek. Prices were modest and made it good value for a night out. Arthur Horner, now in his eighties, recalls visiting the Queen's as a child:

> It was, I think, an independent picture house, and it was not popular. The main entrance was on Stockport Road, but there was an entrance down the side, near the back of the place, for the cheap seats. If you sat in those you got neck ache from looking up. It didn't have a balcony, and the floor sloped upwards from the screen to the dearest seats at the back.

Brian Gregson agrees: 'The Queen's was not the greatest. It had a kind of glass veranda along one side so that people could queue out of the rain.' Of the three Longsight picture houses, the Queen's seems to have been the least liked. Christine Boyall, who was a child in Longsight in the early 1940s, thought the Queen's was 'a ghastly place. It was very downmarket and seemed to have been thrown up.' Dorothy Barron, also a resident of Longsight in the 1930s, thought the Queen's 'very scruffy. There was a rumour, maybe no more than that, that one seat had a rats' nest in it, because the brook ran behind the Queen's.'

Steve Swanell told the author, 'You could always get in at the Queen's for an X film, even if you didn't look eighteen.' This was perhaps one of the reasons why the Queen's equalled the King's and the Shaftesbury in surviving into the 1960s. It finally closed on 21 March

1961, just two months before the Shaftesbury. The last film shown there was the Jules Verne story *Journey to the Centre of the Earth*. The building was eventually demolished and shops occupy the site today.

Graham Todd sheds an interesting light on the Longsight picture houses as they approached the end of their lives:

> I suppose I must have started going to the three cinemas when I was about nine years old in the 1950s. All three were pretty run down by then. The seats were dirty, the paint was flaking off the interior walls, the décor was distinctly drab – dull reds, browns and magnolia. They stunk with the smell of stale cigarette smoke and accumulated dust. The curtains were ragged and torn. The Queen's was built along an unconverted section of Gore Brook, the foul smelling water eventually disappearing into a culvert under Stockport Road. One didn't linger long there – the brook was plagued with large numbers of dirty, emaciated and bedraggled rats, which lived in the culvert and the holes in the steep banks.

Stockport Road leaves Longsight to enter Levenshulme, another heavily built-up area, and, in 2010, a multicultural district. Sixty years ago Levenshulme could boast five picture houses, two of them picture palaces. Yew Tree Avenue branches off Stockport Road on your right, near the centre of Levenshulme. As you walk into Yew Tree Avenue, you will see a single-storey building which, in recent days, has been used as a sports centre. The building, which has been there for almost a century, opened in 1913 as the Arcadia Electric Theatre, its owners being Northern Amusements Ltd. Brian Gregson, now in his eighties, was a patron of the Arcadia in the 1930s:

> All the local kids called it the Ack-a-die-a. It didn't have a balcony. The floor sloped upwards from the screen to the back of the picture house, the dearest seats being those at the back, where there were some double seats for courting couples. The Arcadia had a commissionaire named Percy, who only had one arm. I used to go to the Arcadia on Sunday nights and a fellow used to go who took an alarm clock, which always went off at 7.40 p.m. Percy used to shine a torch along the rows but he never managed to find the man with the alarm clock.

During the war, children could only go in with an adult. Jean Dunn sometimes went to the Arcadia on her own and she recalls:

> I used to go along the queue, clutching my money in my hand, and look for a kind face – usually a woman. Then I would say pleadingly, 'Will you take me in, please, missus?' I'd hand over my money and she would buy the tickets. Once inside we went our separate ways.

Patricia Shaw was born in Burnage and remembers visiting the Levenshulme picture houses, including the Arcadia:

> It was very old. You sat on wooden benches. Every so often they came around spraying disinfectant everywhere. My parents told me not to go to the Arcadia, but I would go there with my friends and tell Mum and Dad I'd been to one of the other ones.

This building, seen here in 2009, once housed the Arcadia picture house, Levenshulme.

Norma Jones states that, 'The Arcadia was a dark building – a flea pit,' and Dennis Coleshill recalls how 'it had a curved roof and gave the impression of being a temporary building. The road to it from Stockport Road was a dirt track.' Apart from the sound effects in the films which it showed, the Arcadia sometimes had additional ones. Walter Pennington remarks, 'It was situated not far from the main Manchester to London railway line. When an express train passed, the sound of the train drowned the sound of the film.'

The Arcadia survived as a picture house until the summer of 1958, closing on 14 July of that year, when it was showing the Elvis Presley film *Loving You* supported by Charlton Heston in *Pony Express*. Since then the building has been used as a cash and carry, and as the Arcadia Sports Centre. Jean Dunn sheds an interesting light on the social mores of the 1950s:

> The Arcadia was the picture house you had to go to on a Sunday night. That was 'picking-up night'. The Arcadia programme finished about 9 p.m. and we would all parade down Stockport Road to Brierly's Milk Bar, on the corner of Alma Street, where we'd spend hours over one drink. People used to come to Levenshulme on Sunday nights from other districts, so there was some fresh blood around.

Just before the junction of Stockport Road and Albert Road, on the right-hand side going towards Stockport, you will find Farmside Place. In 1911 the Electric Picture Palace opened there, managed by Mr J. Harrison. Within a year the seating capacity had been increased from

1,050 to 1,200 – a sure sign that it was a popular place. A later change of name made it the Levenshulme Cinema, and in 1939 it became the Palace. After Mr Harrison's death it was operated by his trustees, which suggests that he was owner/manager. For a time, in the 1940s, it was part of the HDM circuit. Between April and June 1957 the picture house closed for refurbishment, and reopened as the New Palace. It had a much longer life than most cinemas of its kind, showing films into the 1980s. It finally closed on 1 March 1983, going out on a high note with Steven Spielberg's magical *ET*.

A lifetime of seventy-two years as a picture house shows that the Palace was a very popular venue. Most of the people with whom the author discussed Levenshulme said that it was known locally as the Farmside, never the Palace. Although a reasonably sized hall, it only had a small balcony, with some double lovers' seats on the back row. A drawback to its location was that Levenshulme station was just behind it, and you could hear the trains pass by. Dorothy Barron was a child in Levenshulme in the 1930s and her family had close ties with the Palace:

My mother, Florence Reynolds, worked as an usherette at the Palace, becoming cashier in the pay box and later manager. I always had a lot of friends because my mum let us in to the Palace free. Next to the picture house was Burdette's bakery, and, while you were watching the picture, you could smell the bread baking.

Pat Binczak, who was born in Levenshulme but now lives in Leicestershire, remembers the Palace in the 1960s:

The Palace had a children's matinee every Saturday afternoon, and I used to go with my two cousins. They had half a crown [2s 6d] between them, so I used to have 1s 3d. It cost 9d to get in, and, though we were not supposed to go upstairs, I have vivid memories of sitting in the balcony, so we must

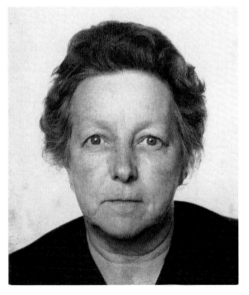

Left: Florence Reynolds – usherette, cashier and finally manager at the Palace, Levenshulme.

Right: PC Eddie Douglas, whose beat was in Levenshulme and who often slipped into the Palace, stood at the back and had a sly cigarette.

The Grand, Levenshulme,
during its demolition.

have sneaked up there. The seats were dark red velvet and had seen better days. We saw mainly
black-and-white pictures and cartoons. There was an interval, and I always had an ice lolly,
which cost 4d. If you were upstairs, the trick was to flick the lolly stick at the kids downstairs
in the second half. As we left the picture house we passed a junk shop in the little street
leading to Stockport Road. It had lots of mismatched pottery outside, and I always spent the
2d I had left on a plate for my mum. I'm sure she was thrilled!

Dorothy and Pat's affectionate memories of the Palace are balanced by those of Walter
Pennington, who made his only visit there with his wife in 1953 to see the film of the Queen's
Coronation: 'That was the first and last time we went to the Palace. My poor wife came out
black and blue with flea bites on her legs.' After the Palace finally closed as a picture house, it
was much altered, and has since been used as a nightclub. The building is one of the few picture
house buildings which still survives. An unusual view of it was provided by Eddy Douglas, a
retired police constable:

I walked a beat along Stockport Road in Levenshulme. As bobbies we were always welcome
at the Palace, and could enjoy a sly fag, standing at the back of the stalls. If we were lucky we
might even get an ice lolly! There was never any trouble, but, if there had been, it would have
done no harm for a bobby to be seen there.

As you go through the Stockport Road – Albert Road junction towards Stockport, on the
left-hand side there is a yawning, boarded-up space between the shops – a space once occupied
by the Grand picture house. Built in 1913, it boasted an impressive frontage, rather like that
of a Southern plantation in films like *Gone with the Wind*. Jean Dunn was certainly impressed:
'The Grand was a nice place. There were steps up to the front entrance and some big pillars,
which made it seem very grand.' It was, though, quite a small place, seating just 687 people.
Dorothy Barron was unimpressed, saying, 'The Grand wasn't very elegant.' Brian Gregson told
the author, 'If you sat on the front row, all you saw was a white line – the front row was so close
to the screen.'

Walter Pennington was astonished the first time he went to the Grand in the 1930s: 'I was
surprised when, at the pay box, I was given not a paper ticket, but a metal disc. You handed this
to the usherette, who threaded it onto a cord.' It is, perhaps, Patricia Shaw's recollection of the
Grand which is the most damning: 'The toilets were off the foyer, and you could smell them as
soon as you went in; they stank!'

The Grand was the first of the Levenshulme picture houses to close its doors. The end came on 2 February 1957, when it was showing a double bill of reissues – James Mason in *The Desert Fox* and Richard Widmark and Marilyn Monroe in *Don't Bother to Knock*. The building was taken over by St Mary's Catholic Church, which used it while a new church was being built. It later became a furniture store and, when that closed, stood empty until it was finally pulled down in November 2005.

The Arcadia, the Palace and the Grand all merit the description 'run of the mill'. The two remaining Levenshulme picture houses, though, could justifiably be called 'picture palaces'. On the other side of Stockport Road, almost opposite the Grand, the ABC circuit opened a new cinema shortly before Christmas 1937. Brian Gregson, a child in Levenshulme in the 1930s, watched the Regal being built. Dorothy Barron, whose father was a projectionist who did a stint at the Regal, calls it 'a real picture palace, the "in" cinema in Levenshulme.'

John Horsfield knew the Regal in the 1940s and thought it 'a very, very fine super cinema, one of the best in Manchester'. With a prominent position alongside a major road, and seating for 1,850 people, the Regal was a success from the start. Patricia Shaw recalls:

It was very modern and there was an organ, which appeared from below the floor before the film started. The Regal was very posh – the place you went to with your parents. If you could afford seats in the rear stalls, it was something.

The Nawaab restaurant, once the Regal picture palace, Levenshulme.

Norma Jones described the Regal as …

> … The poshest one. It had a large foyer, with photos of many big stars on the walls. You always had to queue and there was a commissionaire, who would walk along the queue, calling out, 'Two in the circle, four in the stalls' as seats became available.

Dennis Coleshill remembers 'a beautiful curved staircase up to the circle area'. It seems clear that a visit to the Regal, which ran continuous performances from 6 p.m., as well as daily matinees, was a real event. The cinema could host stage and variety performances too, since it had a stage and four dressing rooms.

As well-remembered as the Regal, by everyone who spoke with this author, is one of its managers – a Mr Sidi. Always immaculately turned out and obviously a showman, he cared about Levenshulme. He inaugurated what he called 'The Levenshulme civic week of happiness' and organised shows, games and parades in the local park. He also organised 'Miss Levenshulme' beauty contests.

The Regal was, without doubt, a classy place and did good business well into the 1950s. In January 1957 a fire in the balcony forced the Regal's closure, while the damage was put right. The cinema reopened in April that same year and continued to provide film entertainment for Levenshulme people until April 1961, when ABC took the decision to close it. That happened on Saturday 22 April, after the final showing of *Saturday Night and Sunday Morning*. The building became a bowling alley – Levenshulme Bowl – but that eventually closed. Today the premises are occupied by the Nawaab International Restaurant.

Unlike the Regal, Levenshulme's other super cinema, which stood on the corner of Kingsway and Moseley Road, is long gone. The Kingsway Super Cinema, opened on 14 March 1929, could almost match the Regal in its seating (1,810) and, like the Regal, was equipped with a stage and six dressing rooms for stage and variety performances. It also boasted a café as one of its attractions, and, again like the Regal, had an organ, which was played in the intervals.

The Kingsway picture palace, Levenshulme, *c.* 1930.

OPEN SESAME

TO-NIGHT'S THE NIGHT

At 6.30 P.M. the doors will open strictly speaking they will open about 5.45 pm the

GREAT NEW WONDER CINEMA OF MANCHESTER

The

KINGSWAY - SUPER CINEMA

West Point, Moseley Road, Levenshulme
Trams from Albert Square and Market street

TO-NIGHT CONTINUOUS from 6.30. Hurry along
Nothing like it in Manchester—the very last
word in Cinema Luxury and Novelty
Prices 6d. 9d. 1/-. 1/3 and 2/6. Hear the
Wonderful CINEMA. REX GLORIA ORGAN.

FILM PROGRAMME

includes two big Pictures you will enjoy
"GLORIOUS BETSY" DOLORES COSTELLO
"GLORIOUS BETSY" DOLORES COSTELLO
"GLORIOUS BETSY" DOLORES COSTELLO
Also CLARA BOW in "RED HAIR"
CLARA BOW in "RED HAIR"
CLARA BOW in "RED HAIR"
Pathe's News Gazette and Eve's Review

KINGSWAY—The New Wonder Cinema
THE BEST WAY THE KINGS WAY
Telephone RUSHOLME DOUBLE TWO DOUBLE ONE

LEVENSHULME

ARCADIA. "Last of the Buccaneers" (U):
Johnny ("Cry") Ray. "Eddie Condon" (U).
GRAND (RUS 1108). Cary Grant, "ROOM FOR
ONE MORE" (U). Cont. 2 p.m. Last show 8.25.
KINGSWAY (A.B.C.). "Sorrowful Jones" (U):
"Thunder in God's Country" (U). L.S. 7.20.
PALACE (H.D.M.). Cont. from 6.0.
Dana Andrews, "ASSIGNMENT PARIS" (U).
REGAL (A.B.C.). Mario Lanza. Doretta Morrow.
"Because You're Mine" (U) (Tech.). L.S. 7.40.

LONGSIGHT

KING'S (H.D.M.). Cont. 6.0. Mat. 2.0.
"SOMEBODY LOVES ME" (U). Tech.
QUEEN'S. 6.0 (Mat. 2.15) Cary Grant. Betsy
Drake. "ROOM FOR ONE MORE" (U).
SHAFTESBURY (H.D.M.). Special Mat. 2. Ct. 6.
Dana Andrews. "ASSIGNMENT PARIS" (U).

An advert for the opening of the Kingsway picture house in 1929, and composite advert for Longsight and Levenshulme picture houses, 1952.

The Kingsway became part of the Union Cinema Group in 1936, but was taken over by ABC a year later, and remained an ABC cinema until its closure. Brian Gregson's mother-in-law had a cake shop on Burnage Lane. She used to put a poster, advertising the Kingsway's programme, in the shop window every week. In return she received two free tickets weekly. Since she didn't go to the pictures, Brian and his wife often used the tickets. The Kingsway stayed in business for almost thirty years. The cinema was showing *Tammy* and *Appointment with a Shadow* – a popular programme – on 25 June 1957, when, during the night, a fire broke out in the building. The huge CinemaScope screen, which was made of fibre glass, partly melted with the heat and so was useless. It is interesting to note that this cinema fire occurred just a few months after the one at the Regal. ABC took the decision to close the cinema and the Kingsway never reopened. The building was eventually demolished and today an office block occupies the site.

SEVEN

RUSHOLME, WITHINGTON, BURNAGE, DIDSBURY, WYTHENSHAWE AND NORTHENDEN

Oxford Road passes Manchester University and Whitworth Park to its junction with Moss Lane East, after which it becomes Wilmslow Road – whose first stretch, in these multi-ethnic days, is commonly referred to as 'The Curry Mile', because of the predominance of Asian restaurants. In the first half of the twentieth century there were three picture houses on this stretch of Wilmslow Road. On the left-hand side of the road leaving Manchester, between Little Western and Great Western Streets, could be found the depot/terminus for the horse-drawn carriages of the Manchester Carriage Co. As motor transport replaced the horse-drawn kind, that building, in 1923, became the home of Rusholme Repertory Theatre, which numbered among its famous players Robert Donat and Alan Badel.

The Rep closed in 1940, and the following year the building reopened as the Rusholme Cinema. Roy Pennill, who knew the area, describes the building:

> The frontage of the building had a veranda and a wide cobbled forecourt, with low railings at the Oxford Road side. The forecourt was obviously designed to accommodate carriages dropping off and picking up theatre-goers. The frontage had always been like this – not at all what you would expect of a traditional cinema.

The Rusholme Cinema was obviously something of a practical landmark. There was a bus stop outside and people would ask for Rusholme Rep or the Rusholme Office (of the Manchester Carriage Co.). Ann Phillips' father had a gents' hairdresser/umbrella repair shop on the corner of Wilmslow Road/Denison Road, almost opposite the Rusholme Cinema. Ann often went to the pictures there with her mother, during the war, because it was so close to home. 'The building was parallel with Wilmslow Road,' Ann recalls. 'You always went into the auditorium through curtained doors, which I imagine were to shut out the light. The seats were parallel with Wilmslow Road, and the screen was at the Moss Lane East end of the building.'

Composite advert for Rusholme, Withington, Burnage, Didsbury, Northenden and Wythenshawe picture houses. The dates on the Coronation and Forum adverts show how the Coronation stole a march with CinemaScope.

The Rusholme Cinema, seating 938 people, was a popular picture house and favourite venue for families. It did good business for nearly thirty years, finally closing on 22 June 1968, when the programme consisted of two 1950s' monster movies, *The Giant Gila Monster* and *The Killer Shrews*. Roy Clark often went to children's matinees at the Rusholme Cinema. They were, by Roy's account, boisterous affairs:

> The Rep seemed to have more breakdowns during children's matinees than any other picture house. This would cause booing, whistling and general mayhem. The staff had their work cut out trying to control us, as we spilled out in the aisles, chasing about and climbing over the seats. As soon as the film started again, quiet descended until the next breakdown.

The building, which housed the Rusholme Cinema, was eventually pulled down.

A little further along Wilmslow Road, a picture house with 1,000 seats opened on the corner of Moor Street (no longer there) in 1912. This became the Trocadero picture house and operated on that site for more than sixty years, though the number of seats was reduced to 850 later. The building, nestling between the shops of Wilmslow Road, had an impressive frontage, a tower above the entrance and an arched arcade; later the name Trocadero was spelled out in large letters across the front. A single-storey building, it had no balcony. There was a long foyer and the pay box at the front, on Wilmlow Road, and another down the side street for the cheaper seats. The arcade sheltered the people in the queue from the rain, and contained two shops, one either side of the picture house entrance. Local people always referred to the Trocadero as the Troc. Roy Pennill often went to the Trocadero in the 1930s:

> The ticket was cheap, and, while it wasn't the best decorated of cinemas, it was always clean and comfortably warm. It seemed to have none of the draughts usually found in other picture houses. The building had its own – not unpleasant – odour, probably due to the use of gas lamps for the subdued, low-level lighting around the walls. The Troc was a popular place with courting couples, because it was warm and quiet.

The Trocadero opened six nights a week. It did not begin Sunday shows until very late on in its life. Weeknight performances were continuous and on Saturdays there were two separate shows. If there was a big queue on a Saturday, the manager would not start the show until everyone was seated. Roy Clark thought the Trocadero 'one of the better class picture houses. It was neat, clean, very comfortable and well organised. No matter where you sat you had a good view of the screen.'

Because the Trocadero often showed films which had done the rounds a few months earlier, people got the chance to catch good pictures, perhaps missed first time around, and this added to its attraction. Ann Phillips, who lived across the road, often went to the Trocadero in her teens. She has fond memories of the lady in the pay box there: 'The cash desk lady, who had been there for years would say, "Oh, my friend hasn't come tonight. You may have her free pass." So I rarely had to pay.' In February 1963 the Trocadero closed for modernising, but it soon reopened, and continued in business until Monday, 15 September 1975. That week it was showing *Around the World with Fanny Hill* and *The Case of the Smiling Stiff*. On the Monday night a fire broke out and did a lot of damage. The Trocadero closed and never reopened. Some time later the building was demolished.

Rusholme's third picture house, also on Wilmslow Road, was, by some way, the district's grandest. There had been a cinema on the site as early as 1916, which had closed, then reopened in the early 1920s. The Casino, as it was called, stayed open then for almost forty years. It was owned by a man named Ben Kanter, but, on 1 July 1929, it became part of the ABC circuit, and later became known as the ABC Casino. Roy Clark recalls that the Casino was situated opposite Dickenson Road. It opened seven nights a week, with two performances daily and one on Sundays. Like most of the picture houses taken over by ABC, the Casino was a large place, seating 1,420 patrons. It was also, like most ABC cinemas, a posh place. Ann Phillips remembers:

> There were marble steps up to the entrance, and shops either side of the entrance. One of them was, I think, a dress shop. When I was a teenager, I used to go in the Dress Circle seats, and an usherette always showed me to the same seat.

Rusholme theatre in the early years of the twentieth century. (Courtesy of Cinema Theatre Association archive)

The Trocadero picture house, Rusholme, 1959. (Courtesy of Manchester Archives and Local Studies, Central Library)

The Casino picture house, Rusholme, *c.* 1930. (Courtesy of Cinema Theatre Association, Tony Moss Collection)

The ABC Casino, well situated and with access to the ABC circuit releases which starred many of the most popular actors – Gable, Garbo, Robert Taylor, Crawford, Jeanette MacDonald and Nelson Eddy all graced ABC screens – was a very popular venue. Like most ABC cinemas it ran a Saturday morning children's matinee. The boys would be running round, yelling and carrying on, and the manager – not very tall but well-rounded – having ordered the film to be turned off, would go up on the stage and threaten, 'If you lot don't behave, you are going home.' The ABC Casino continued in business until 20 October 1960, when it was showing *In the Nick* and *Because They're Young*. That night a fire in the building took hold quickly and the Casino was badly damaged. It never reopened as a picture house and was eventually pulled down.

CAUGHT OUT

The Casino Rusholme had a ballroom. One lady interviewed for this book had this story to tell:

I was going out with a sailor. One of my fellow workers at Trafford Park invited me on a date on New Year's Eve. Since my sailor was away, I accepted. Shortly before New Year's Eve I received news that the sailor was coming home on leave. I told my co-worker that I couldn't go out with him because a close relative had died. On New Year's Eve my sailor boyfriend and I went to the Casino at Rusholme to the ballroom. We were happily climbing the stairs to the dance hall, when who should we meet coming down but the co-worker I had brushed off. He didn't say a word, but I was really embarrassed. And he never spoke to me again.

Wilmslow Road skirts Fallowfield, eventually becomes Palatine Road and enters Withington, once home to two picture houses – the Palatine on Palatine Road, and the Scala in the town centre.

The Scala Electric Palace, a small building seating 634 people, opened before the First World War and, with no close competition, flourished. Programmes changed on Thursdays and were continuous Monday to Friday; Saturdays had two separate shows. On 1 October 1940, a bomb fell in the street outside the Scala – by which name it was popularly known – damaging the picture house and necessitating its closure. The damage was quickly repaired and the Scala reopened on 20 October 1940 – the seating reduced to 600. Through the 1950s and '60s, when picture houses were closing in large numbers all over Manchester, the Scala continued, amazingly lasting almost to the end of the twentieth century. In February 1980 it underwent a dramatic change. Alterations were made to the interior and, on 18 February 1980, the Scala began operating as a twin cinema, advertised as Scala 1 and 2. The opening films were *Star Trek* in Scala 1 and *The Rescuers* in Scala 2. A week or so later Scala 3 opened with a film called *Last Feelings*. In the new complex, Scala 1 seated 130 people, Scala 2 143, and Scala 3 154. Some time later the picture house's name was changed to Cine City. Michaela Wilcox went to Saturday morning children's shows there and remembers it as 'a tiny place with single, double and triple red velvet seats. It cost £1.25 to get in.'

Cine City lasted until 1997, when the owner took the decision to close the complex. In 2001 the site was sold to a new owner. The intention was to demolish the old Scala and the pub next door and redevelop the site. However, after representations from Withington Civic Society, the new owner agreed to let them try to raise the funds to refurbish the picture house and reopen for films. Their valiant efforts came to nothing, alas; it was an impossible task. The Scala has since been demolished. Plans put forward, including an arts complex in the development, were not approved. In 2009, when this author visited Withington to look at the derelict building, shortly before it was demolished, an elderly lady who was passing by said, quite unprompted, 'I went there as a child. It was a beautiful picture house, always a pleasure to visit. They ruined it when they made all those little ones.'

Withington's other picture house, along Palatine Road, on the way to Didsbury, was the Palatine Picture House, a large hall seating 1,034 people, which opened in 1920. Margaret Bruce, who knew the building, described it as, 'A not very prepossessing building, just one storey.' One of its attractions, however, was its café, which was included in the name of the picture house, which adorned the side of the building – the Palatine Picture House and Café. The original owners were South Manchester Picture Theatre Co., but, by the late 1930s, the Palatine had become part of the HDM circuit.

Although three other picture houses were quite near – the Scala Withington, the Forum Wythenshawe, and the Coronation Northenden – the Palatine managed to stay in business for some forty years. It closed on Saturday, 26 March 1960, after the final showing of *Please Turn Over* (a comedy starring comedian Ted Ray) and *The Desperate Man*. The building remained for some time, before it was eventually demolished.

Of the southern districts of Manchester, Burnage was unusual in having only one picture house, albeit a splendid one. The Lido, a super cinema owned by Anglo-Scottish Cinemas and seating 1,560 people, opened in 1928 at the junction of Kingsway and Green End Road in the Kingsway Buildings. It had a stage and several dressing rooms, as well as a café and a

Cine City (formerly Scala), Withington, 2009, shortly before demolition.

The Palatine Picture House and Café, Withington.

ballroom. Edie Douglas recalls: 'It was a large building. It had a balcony, and I did most of my courting there.'

Kathleen Wardle lived on Green End Road, next door to the Lido. She and her family had connections with the cinema. When Kathleen was a child she often went there with her mum, and when she was thirteen she joined the committee for the Saturday morning kids' shows. Kathleen used to play her accordion. She was friendly with a boy, who used to sing and tell jokes at the children's shows and lived nearby with his dad and his younger brother. He was John Thaw – years later television's Inspector Morse. Kathleen's mother became a cleaner at the Lido and her brother a projectionist. Kathleen recalls:

> When I was eighteen, I worked at the Lido as an usherette. I had an important job. Every evening I had to take the newsreel from the Lido to the Capitol in Parr's Wood Road. I had to wait until they had shown it, then take it back to the Lido for the following evening.

It was inevitable that a picture palace like the Lido would attract the attention of the big circuits. Rank bought the Lido in 1942. It retained the name for a while, but in 1945 it became the Odeon, Burnage, and provided first-class film entertainment for local people for some twenty years. Rank, rationalising its cinema chain, took the decision to close it in December 1967, when it was showing *The Sand Pebbles* starring Steve McQueen. Rank had already sold the building, however, and it reopened the next day, 10 December, as the Classic. The opening film was *Robbery*.

Classic operated the picture house until July 1971, at which point it became simply the Cinema. On 30 September, the *Manchester Evening News* carried an article saying that a man named Geoffrey Henshaw – who, as a child, had attended the Saturday Cartoon Club at the Odeon – had taken over the building. Alterations were made, turning the circle into a 400-seat cinema, the Concorde, and the stalls area into a bingo hall. The new complex was known as Burnage Entertainment Centre. Two years or so later the Concorde was twinned, becoming Concorde 1 and 2. That arrangement lasted for ten years until January 1984, when one of the screens was closed. Eight months later, on 30 September 1984, the whole complex closed, and eventually became a Kwik Save supermarket. Later, part of the supermarket was destroyed by fire and the whole building was eventually demolished. In 2010, that prime site is occupied by an Aldi supermarket.

Kingsway connects in Didsbury with School Lane, once the location of one of Didsbury's two picture houses – the Capitol. Originally owned by Union Cinemas, the Capitol opened

The Odeon (formerly Lido), Burnage, 1952.

The Capitol picture house, Didsbury, 1930s.

on 21 May 1931. Less than a year later, on 25 April 1932, fire destroyed the auditorium, resulting in the building's demolition. The original architect, Peter Cummings, designed a new picture house, which opened on 16 August 1933. The original Capitol had 1,900 seats – 1,400 in the stalls and 500 in the circle. The new building had an organ, a stage and eight dressing rooms, which meant it could be used for stage performances. A café had also been included in the first Capitol, but not in its successor. Performances were continuous every evening, and there was a matinee daily at 2 p.m.

In 1937 the Union cinemas joined the ABC circuit, and the Capitol remained with ABC until the end of its life. Claire Norman has good memories of the Capitol. Her mother, Margaret Henthorne, was an usherette there in the late 1930s, and Margaret often told Claire stories about the picture house. When it became an ABC cinema, the seating capacity of the Capitol was slightly reduced – to 1,838.

The cinema did good business for twenty years, until it was closed quite abruptly in 1956. The last films shown there were *I Am a Camera* and *Angela*. After closure on 14 December 1956, the building was immediately converted to studios for ABC TV, whose main studios were in Birmingham. Some popular television programmes, including Hughie Green's *Opportunity Knocks*, were broadcast from the Didsbury studios. When ABC had no further use for the building, the Drama Department of Manchester University took it over for drama courses. When they ended, the building was demolished. The housing, which replaced it, is called Capitol Court.

Elm Grove, in Didsbury's centre, is also the site of some new housing – though it was once the location of the Bijou Picture Theatre, which opened before the First World War. It later became the Didsbury Picture House and even later the Didsbury Theatre. Then, on 31 December 1951, it took its last name – the Tudor – and the first films shown there were *The Milkman* and *Traveller's Joy*. Margaret Bruce has vivid memories of the Tudor:

> I grew up in Didsbury. My mother would take me to the Tudor cinema after school and after tea on a Friday. We would see and enjoy the films – musicals were our favourites – and on our way home Mum bought fish and chips. I have always been allergic to fish, so I used to get chips and peas. I remember having a terrible nightmare after we had been to see *Great Expectations*.

Margaret Henthorne, Mary Mooney and Betty Willie: usherettes at the Capitol, Didsbury, *c.* 1938.

After the demise of the Capitol, the Tudor was Didsbury's sole picture house for more than ten years. It closed on 12 August 1967, when it was showing the Julie Christie film *Fahrenheit 451.* The bingo hall, which replaced it, later closed and the building remained empty for some time until it was demolished for new housing.

Northenden and Wythenshawe are Manchester's two most southerly districts. Just before Princess Parkway, Longley Lane joins Palatine Road. Maps indicate the area is in Northenden. For many years there were two picture houses in this area; one was a modest house on Longley Lane, the other was a real picture palace which was located on Palatine Road, opposite where Longley Lane joins it. In the *Manchester Evening News* entertainment pages, the Longley Lane house was advertised as the Coronation in Northenden; the Forum, however, was in Wythenshawe – strange, since they cannot have been more than a couple of hundred yards apart.

The Public Hall opened on Longley Lane in 1911. In 1918 it became the Electric Picture Theatre and in 1930 the Royal Electric Theatre. Peter Leigh, who owned it, also owned the pub next door, the Farmer's Arms. Roy Pennill used to go to the picture house between 1937 and 1941: 'It was just a wooden structure, an austere place, named locally "the bug hut". I seem to remember it was also used sometimes for wrestling.'

From 1937 the name of the picture house was changed to the Coronation – perhaps to mark the Coronation of King George VI and Queen Elizabeth. Bryant (Tony) Hill, who was born in 1933, remembers:

> The Coronation was built as some kind of memorial hall. When it began as a picture house it had no screen; the film was projected onto the wall. It was a single-storey building and the floor was hardly ramped. If you had someone tall in front of you it was difficult to see the picture. The seats at the front were just hard benches, but there were some lovers' double seats on the back row.

The author, searching for any picture house buildings which still remain, visited Northenden and had a drink in the Farmer's Arms. Two female customers confirmed that locals had called the Coronation a 'bug hut'. Another very elderly lady told me that she had a long association with pub and picture house:

> I was only sixteen when I came to Northenden to work in the Farmer's Arms. I also lived there. The Leighs, who owned the pub, also owned the picture house next door. On my days off I used to get into the Coronation for free.

The Coronation continued to show films well into the 1960s, before succumbing, as did so many, to bingo. It closed on Saturday, 22 February 1964, after the last showing of *Fury of the Vikings* and *Women by Night*. Bingo continued for some time but, when that finished, the building was left to decay, until it was finally demolished in the 1980s. The pub car park now occupies the site.

In contrast to the Coronation – a very modest picture house, with an almost spartan interior – its near neighbour, at the corner of Longley Lane and Palatine Road, was a true picture palace. The Forum, which opened in 1934, was much more than just a place to see movies. It also boasted a café, a ballroom, a stage and dressing rooms; this facilitated stage shows, including a pantomime, each year. Stalls and a circle provided a total seating capacity of 1,904, and, in the intervals between films, customers were entertained by a Wurlitzer organ. Bryant (Tony) Hill lived in Wythenshawe in his childhood and has good memories of the Forum:

> I often went to the Forum as a child. It was a lovely place; there was a large foyer from which two sweeping staircases led to the café and the circle. When I left school in July 1948, the manager, Mr Lyons (who knew me and was aware of my interest in films), offered me a job at the Forum as a trainee projectionist. I worked my way up to third operator. We hosted lots of stage shows and, while I was there, staged the pantomime 'Aladdin'. I worked at the Forum for three years, only leaving because my then girlfriend complained that she never saw me in the evenings.

Like the other palatial picture houses in Manchester – the Lido Burnage and the Riviera Cheetham Hill – the Forum quickly attracted the attention of the big cinema circuits. In 1936 it became the ABC Forum Wythenshawe, and was thus advertised until 1964, when, in common with the other ABC picture houses, it became simply the ABC Wythenshawe.

An imposing building on a main road, the Forum had no difficulty attracting patrons and stayed in business until the mid-1970s. ABC finally decided to close it on 23 February 1974, and its last film was the Bruce Lee martial arts epic *Fist of Fury*. Nearly forty years later the building still stands proudly on Palatine Road, the exterior the most perfectly preserved of all the Manchester picture houses of the golden age; today it is the meeting hall of the Jehovah's Witnesses.

The Forum picture house,
Wythenshawe, 1953.

Bryant (Tony) Hill, shortly before
leaving school and joining staff of
the Forum, Wythenshawe, as trainee
projectionist.

STEALING A MARCH ON THE COMPETITION

In the whole of Manchester there were no two neighbouring picture houses as different as the Coronation in Northenden and the Forum in Wythenshawe – the former was small and rather tatty, the latter huge and luxurious. Big and beautiful, though, was not always best.

In 1953, Twentieth Century Fox introduced widescreen to the cinema. *The Robe*, the first production filmed in CinemaScope, was an instant success. City centre picture houses, then local ones, rushed to install CinemaScope screens – the Miracle Mirror Screen as it was described – to attract the huge audiences which turned out for early CinemaScope epics like *The Egyptian*, *Knights of the Round Table*, *The Black Shield of Falworth*, *Demetrius and the Gladiators*.

It was 1955 before ABC decided to install CinemaScope in the Forum. For some weeks in January/February 1955 the local paper carried adverts for the Forum with a special addition – that CinemaScope would open shortly with *Three Coins in the Fountain*. Flyers were also published in the paper, simply saying CinemaScope, the Forum and a date: 28 February. This campaign must have cost ABC quite a lot of money. Then, in the week of 14 February, when the local paper came out, the Forum advert was still announcing *Three Coins in the Fountain* in CinemaScope for 28 February. Directly next to it the Coronation advertised for 21 February, 'Now with CinemaScope and Miracle Mirror Screen', *Knights of the Round Table*. The Coronation's owners had stolen a huge march on the Forum by having a CinemaScope screen and projector installed in the Coronation surreptitiously, so that they could show CinemaScope a week before the Forum did – a master stroke of tactics. One can only imagine that the manager of the ABC and his employers were left grinding their teeth. Big is not always best, or first!

EIGHT

CHORLTON-CUM-HARDY, OLD TRAFFORD AND WHALLEY RANGE

Chorlton-cum-Hardy, Old Trafford and Whalley Range cluster together in the south of Manchester. In Chorlton-cum-Hardy, Manchester Road becomes Barlow Moor Road, and the district's three picture houses were once to be found there – one on Manchester Road and the other two on Barlow Moor Road. The first of the three to open (in May 1914), near the junction of Barlow Moor Road and Beech Road, was the Palais De Luxe – its name until the late 1940s, when it became simply the Palace. A fairly large house, seating 1,200 people, its programmes were continuous in the evenings with a Saturday matinee. Derek Eccles, who lived in Chorlton-cum-Hardy as a youngster, remembers the Palace:

> It was a small place; you could book seats for Saturday evenings. There was a doorman who had a day job with the local council. He wore a really ill-fitting uniform, but we kids always felt that he thought he was the bee's knees.

Carol Simcock also remembers the Palace: 'I'm now sixty-two, but, when I was a very young girl, my parents took my sisters and me to the Palace cinema, which was fondly known in the area as "the bug hut".' The Palace, a popular place well into the 1950s, finally closed its doors as a picture house on 4 December 1957, after the final showing of the western *The Lonely Man*, supported by *Lost Treasure of the Amazon*. The building, today a Co-op supermarket, still stands on Barlow Moor Road. Sheila Hatton, who lived in Chorlton-cum-Hardy as a girl, has affectionate memories of the Palace:

> We used to go to Saturday morning pictures. We saw a lot of cowboy pictures, with stars like Roy Rogers and Gene Autry. Afterwards we'd run to the Rec, a kind of park lower down Beech Road, and hide in the bushes, shooting guns at each other, just like the cowboys in the films did.

About three quarters of a mile away from the Palace, by the junction of Nicolas Street and Manchester Road at the other end of Chorlton-cum-Hardy, the Picture House opened in

This supermarket in Chorlton-cum-Hardy was once the Palace picture house.

1920. In 1921 it was leased by Savoy Cinemas, and renamed the Savoy. In 1928 it was taken over by ABC, which operated it for the next eighteen years until, in 1946, it became part of the Gaumont chain and, for the rest of its life was the Gaumont. A large house, it could seat 1,500 people when it was an ABC, though the seating was reduced to 1,250 by Gaumont. The Gaumont's advantageous position, alongside a main road in a heavily-populated area, ensured good business for nearly two decades. Like most picture houses, it ran Saturday morning shows for kids.

The Gaumont, though, has a greater claim to fame than most. The Gibb brothers, Barry, Robin and Maurice, came to live in Manchester in 1955. The three boys went to the Gaumont Saturday morning shows and, on one occasion, were supposed to mime to one of the hit songs of the day before the film started. However, the equipment broke down and they actually sung – one of their earliest performances. The Gaumont continued as a picture house until Rank, in its rationalisation programme in 1962, decided to close some of its Gaumont houses. The Gaumont in Chorlton-cum-Hardy was among them and closed its doors as a cinema on 6 January 1962. The final programme was a double bill of reissues, Doris Day in *The Pajama Game* and *The Charge at Feather River*. The building was bought by the Co-op and, with a considerable change of frontage, became the Co-op Funeral Service. One of those interviewed for this book commented succinctly, 'I liked it much better as the Gaumont!'

Chorlton-cum-Hardy's third picture house, and the one with the most dramatic life, was – like the Palace – at the opposite end of the district on Barlow Moor Road. The Rivoli

Composite advert for the Imperial Brooks Bar, the
Gaumont, and the Essoldo, Chorlton-cum-Hardy.

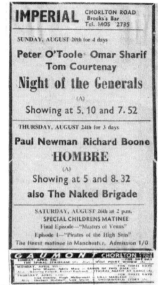

– a large house, almost a picture palace – opened
on 20 November 1936. Derek Eccles lived in
Chorlton-cum-Hardy when it was being built and
saw it open:

> It was an art-deco building, with steps leading up to
> the pay box. It had a large foyer, with pictures of stars
> and posters for coming attractions, and was unusual
> in having both stalls and circle. There were shops on
> either side of the entrance on Barlow Moor Road,
> one side a wool shop, the other a sweet shop.

The Rivoli was just in its fourth year when, in
December 1940, Manchester was blitzed by
German bombers. A bomb landed in the street
outside the picture house and, as Derek Eccles
recalls, 'the front of the cinema was blown away
and you could see right back to the screen.'
The Rivoli was too badly damaged to reopen,
and an armed soldier was put on guard outside
the building, which was requisitioned by the
Ministry of Food and used for the rest of the
war years – presumably with a new frontage. For
Derek and other youngsters, the bomb damage
had both up and down sides:

> When the bomb exploded, the sweet shop was damaged. Sweets were scattered all over the
> street. Kids came from miles around to scavenge for sweets. [But] we had been watching the
> serial in the Saturday morning kids' show; it was *The Mark of Zorro*. At the end of the episode
> Zorro jumped his horse over a chasm. We were all agog to see if he made it the next week –
> but next week never came. The bomb came instead.

Some years after the war ended the Rivoli was rebuilt, reopening on 17 November
1954. Five months later it was taken over by the Essoldo group and became the Essoldo,
Chorlton-cum-Hardy. Essoldo operated it for seventeen years, but sold it to the Classic chain
in April 1972. The Classic, as it was now called, operated as a single-screen cinema for a year or
so before being tripled. The tripled cinema opened on 23 November 1973, with Screen 1 (400
seats) showing *The Day of the Jackal*, Screen 2 (196 seats) showing *The Sound of Music* and Screen
3 (192 seats) *Man at the Top*. The tripling gave the picture house a four and a half year extension
to its life, but Screen 3, which was showing *The Other Side of Midnight*, closed on 15 April 1978
to become a skateboard centre. Screen 2 closed on 15 December 1978. Screen 1 lasted a few

The Savoy, later Gaumont, Chorlton-cum-Hardy. (Courtesy of Cinema Theatre Association, Tony Moss Collection)

The Essoldo (formerly Rivoli), Chorlton-cum-Hardy. (Courtesy of Manchester Archives and Local Studies, Central Library)

The former Imperial Brooks Bar in 2010.

months longer, till March 1979, when Classic sold it. It reopened as the Shalimar, showing Asian films; that lasted until 1982, when the Shalimar too closed. The building has since been demolished and shops built on the site.

Brooks Bar is at the junction of Moss Lane West and Chorlton Road; local people would say that the area is Old Trafford, today synonymous with Manchester United. Sixty years ago cinema rivalled football as mass entertainment. On the right-hand side of Chorlton Road, just before its junction with Withington Road, stood the Imperial picture house. For years the Imperial was advertised in the *Manchester Evening News* entertainment pages as being in Chorlton-cum-Hardy. Only in its last years was it the Imperial Brooks Bar. The Imperial Picture Theatre And Café opened in 1914, under the ownership of Cinemas (Manchester) Ltd; a modestly sized house, seating 760 people, it had no circle but was equipped for live performances. Les Kershaw, now aged seventy-one, recalls:

> The Imperial had two entrances: the main one on Chorlton Road, with an impressive frontage, the other round the corner down the side. Presumably the main one was for the dearer seats, the other for the cheap seats at the front. The usherettes would go round in the interval spraying disinfectant.

Because the Imperial occupied a good position at the junction of several main roads, it easily attracted paying customers. Performances were twice nightly with a matinee on Monday, Wednesday and Saturday. The Imperial survived all the changing phases of cinema – silents, the coming of talkies, the widescreen, and the sex, violence and foul language prevalent in the 1970s. Joan Rees went to live in Charlton as a nine-year-old and later took her son to the Imperial:

> It was a very small place. We used to go there to see Elvis Presley pictures, and my son, with most of the other boys, would dance and wiggle his hips like Elvis. He is still a staunch fan today. It could be bedlam, but the usherettes always had it under control.

The Imperial lasted longer than most picture houses, finally closing on 15 January 1976 – a Thursday – when it was showing the Alistair MacLean adventure story *Caravan to Vaccares* supported by *A Murder is a Murder*. The building still stands on Chorlton Road; from the outside it is without doubt an old picture house, but today a brand new sign proclaims 'Imperial Timber and Building Merchants'.

The Imperial's nearest neighbour was a few hundred yards away along Chorlton Road, on Cornbrook Street. General opinion seems to have been that the Imperial was 'a nice little picture house'. Not so, however, its neighbour the Globe, for which the kindest words were 'bug hut'. The Manchester Carriage Co., at the beginning of the twentieth century, operated horse-drawn buses and trams all over Manchester; one of its depots was in Old Trafford. Part of the depot there eventually became a picture house. The New Globe Picture Hall opened in 1914, its owners being North Western Entertainments Ltd. It was a fairly large picture house, seating 1,230 people. For years, however, the first ten rows were long wooden benches. Joan Rees is very blunt on the subject of the Globe:

We called it a bug hut. The front rows were not seats, just wooden benches. They used to pack in as many people as they could – just like sardines in a tin. It cost just 2*d* to get in [in the 1940s].

The Globe, one of whose managers was quaintly named Trueman Towers, lasted only into the 1950s. Perhaps there is a hint of an explanation for its demise in this comment from John Briggs, who lived in the area from the time he was two years old: 'The Globe was a real bug hut. My mum told me, "If you go in there, I'll break your bleeding neck."' The Globe's huge size and less than salubrious reputation made it difficult to keep going as a viable concern, even when it was part of the HDM circuit in the late 1930s to early 1940s. It finally gave up the ghost on Sunday, 31 March 1957, with a western *Son of Belle Starr* and *Private Eyes*. The building was later demolished.

The Trafford picture house opened on Talbot Road in 1923, under the management of Mr E. Boultbee. With an impressive frontage and 1,200 seats (a number reduced slightly over the years) it was more than just a 'bug hut' and soon attracted the attention of the leading circuits. It became part of ABC just after the war, and it remained an ABC cinema for the rest of its working life. Its good position on a major road, and the fact that it was rather more up-market than most of its local neighbours, ensured it good audiences and the ABC release programme was a great help. Evening performances, and those from 2 p.m. Saturday, were continuous and there were two matinees weekly. However, in November 1958, rather earlier than one would have expected, ABC decided to close it, and its last films were *The Moonraker* and *Orders to Kill* on 30 November. The building was later pulled down.

Opening advert (in 1930) for the West End, later Odeon, in Whalley Range.

The West End, later Odeon, Whalley Range. (Courtesy of Cinema Theatre Association, Tony Moss Collection)

Chorlton Road continues onto Withington Road in Whalley Range. A few hundred yards beyond Brooks Bar stood another of Manchester's picture palaces. Opened on 30 August 1930 as the West End, it was an immediate success. It seated 1,032 people, with a stage and dressing rooms for live performances, and a café. Performances were continuous Monday to Friday, with matinees Saturdays and holidays. The eyes of the main cinema chains – Odeon, Gaumont and ABC – were soon drawn to the magnificent building and its advantageous situation on Withington Road.

The West End became part of the Odeon chain on 30 August 1937, exactly seven years after it opened, and was renamed Odeon Whalley Range, under which name it operated for the remainder of its life. Rank did not take over established picture houses without good reason, and the few Manchester houses which bore the Odeon name – in Cheetham Hill, Burnage and Whalley Range – were the area's most luxurious picture houses. General opinion, among those who were interviewed for this book, was that the Odeon in Whalley Range was 'a lovely place, a real picture palace'. Even such magnificent places, though, were not immune to the falling attendances and extensive closures of the late 1950s and early 1960s. When Rank carried out an extensive cull of its houses in the early 1960s, the Odeon Whalley Range was one of those to go. It closed on Saturday, 23 December 1961, its final programme being a British comedy *No My Darling Daughter* and *Murder in Eden*.

Rank reopened the building on 27 December as the Top Rank Bingo and Social Club. Later called Star Bingo, and later still EMI Bingo, its final closure came in 1980. In 1986 the building was demolished and today Crystal House, a block of flats, occupies the site.

NINE

GORTON

Gorton and Openshaw, two of Manchester's most heavily-populated areas, lie next to each other east of the city. When movies were the most popular form of mass entertainment, between the two world wars and into the 1950s, Gorton and Openshaw were home to no fewer than fourteen picture houses – seven in each area.

Gorton was divided into Gorton and West Gorton: Gorton extending from the Denton boundary to Belle Vue, West Gorton from Belle Vue to Ardwick. Gorton had three picture houses. Two of them opened in 1916, at the height of the First World War. The Cosmo Picture House opened on Wellington Street, behind the Plough pub. Its first owners were Union Cinemas, who sold out to Circuit Cinemas Ltd. Then, in the 1930s, the Cosmo was taken over by ABC.

A modestly sized building, the Cosmo had a balcony, accessed by stairs from the foyer. Frank Rhodes, born and brought up in Gorton, remembers the red plush seating. He often went to the Cosmo in the 1950s: 'I went there with my dad, whenever a western was showing. I swear we came out of the place rubbing our eyes, which were stinging from all the dust that was kicked up by the horses.'

When the Cosmo became part of the ABC circuit, its access to ABC's releases ensured good business through the 1950s. Jean Wheeldon lived as a child on Brown Street, later Dorney Street, around the corner from the Cosmo. Jean recalls:

Jean Wheeldon and her mum in the garden of their home, round the corner from the Cosmo where they were frequent visitors.

CONWAY BINGO & SOCIAL CLUB

CLOWES STREET, WEST GORTON

AFTERNOON SESSIONS DAILY

Sundays and Saturdays — Doors open 2-30 p.m. — Eyes down 3 p.m.
Monday to Friday — Doors open 1-30 p.m. — Eyes down 2 p.m.

FREE ! FREE ! FREE !
BOOKS

PLAY AS MANY AS YOU LIKE
ADMISSION 5/-. PLUS FREE GAME

MONDAY NEXT MAY 27

Business as usual during afternoon filming of
GRANADA TELEVISION SERIES of "CITY '68"

EVENING SESSIONS

Doors open 7-45 p.m. — Eyes down 8 p.m.
SUNDAY — PLAY AS MANY BOOKS AS YOU LIKE
ADMISSION 5/-
MONDAY/WEDNESDAY — 8 HOUSE BOOK 2/-
ADMISSION 1/6
THURSDAY/SATURDAY — 10 HOUSE BOOK 3/-
ADMISSION 2/-

3d. QUICKIE "BOTTLE" GAME PLAYED EVERY EVENING

BIG CASH PRIZES TO BE WON ON
WEEKEND FLYER — FRIDAY, SATURDAY, SUNDAY

GORTON

CORONA. Rory Calhoun, Piper Laurie.
"Ain't Misbehaving" (U) (Tech.). Sun.,
"Bedtime For Bonzo": "The Adventurers."
COSMO (A.B.C.). C. 5 55. "Many Rivers to
Cross" (U). "The Affairs of Dr. Holl" (A).
Sun., Ct. 2 30: 'Lost Stage Valley' (U). Tech.
ESSOLDO. Bing Crosby, Grace Kelly, William
Holden. "THE COUNTRY GIRL" (A).
"THE BLACK FOREST" (A).. Sun.
William Holden, "STREETS OF LAREDO"
(U). Tech.: "VARIETIES ON PARADE."
OLYMPIA. C. 6. Cinemascope, Technicolor.
Edmund Purdom. "STUDENT PRINCE."
PLAZA. Cont. 6 5. "HEIDI," a children's
story Venice Award Film. 1953. Sunday:
Maureen O'Hara. "BAGDAD."

Composite advert for Gorton picture houses in 1955, and the demise of the Conway to bingo.

The Cosmo picture house in the mid-1950s. (Courtesy of Cinema Theatre Association archive)

We went to the Cosmo on Monday night and Saturday night. If we had thunder and lightning, Mum used to be terrified. She used to run and get our coats and say, 'Come on, we're going to the Cosmo.' We would stay there till the storm had passed.

Sometimes, if the film had an A certificate – which meant children had to be accompanied by an adult – the lady in the pay box wouldn't let youngsters in unaccompanied. On one occasion, Jean and her cousin, Sue, were refused admission. Sue said, 'Let's dress up in your mum's clothes. They'll let us in then.' So the two girls put on Jean's mum's best clothes and the pay box lady still wouldn't let them in! ABC operated the Cosmo – the Cosy Cos, as it was affectionately known – until summer of 1960, when they decided to close it. The last programme, on 1 August 1960, was the Abbott and Costello comedy *Dance With Me, Henry* and a western, *Fort Yuma*. Notices appeared advising patrons to watch for the reopening date, but it seems never to have reopened as a picture house. The building has since had various uses, among them a bike shop and a fishing tackle shop. Finally left derelict, it was demolished in late 2008 when a new Tesco store was built.

IT'S FRANKENSTEIN! HE'S COMING TO GET US!

Frank Rhodes' dad suffered from polio as a child. Doctors thought his legs would have to be amputated, but managed to save them. However, one was slightly shorter than the other, so he had to wear a built-up shoe, which made a clunking noise as he walked. One night he had been to the Cosmo to see the classic Karloff horror picture *Frankenstein*. As he walked home two girls were ahead of him. They had to cross a bridge which was made of wooden sleepers. As Mr Rhodes crossed the bridge, his built-up shoe made loud clunking noises. The two girls, looking nervously behind them, screamed in terror, 'It's Frankenstein! He's coming to get us,' and ran like the wind to get away.

On Hyde Road – the main road through Gorton – about a hundred yards from the Cosmo, the Olympia Picture House, owned by Gorton and District Cinemas Ltd, opened in 1920. It had no balcony but the stalls area, seating 750 people, sloped upwards towards the back, where the seats were more expensive. Weekday performances were continuous, but Saturdays had three shows. The Olympia was also equipped for live shows. It closed in 1927, but reopened and became simply the Olympia. Frank Raven remembers that it was 'a bit run down, with rickety seats', but it was refurbished in the 1950s. Frank Rhodes thought it was 'a posher place than the Cosmo'.

The Olympia did have one feature that almost all of the Gorton people interviewed for this book mentioned. In most cinemas, on entering you paid your money and were given a paper ticket, which you handed to the usherette who tore it in half, gave one half back to you and threaded the other onto a long string. At the Olympia, you paid and were given a metal disc. You handed this to the usherette, who dropped it into a metal fire bucket. The clanking noise as the disc hit the metal could be heard all over the picture house when anybody entered the auditorium – a great distraction when you were lost in the happenings on the screen. The

Frank Rhodes, film fan and frequenter of Gorton picture houses.

Olympia got by very well for years on a diet of reissues, or films having a second run in Gorton. Frank Raven recalls:

> One of our neighbours lived in an end terrace house, and a poster board for the Olympia was attached to the side wall of the house. It contained the Olympia's weekly programme. For that the owners got free tickets to the Olympia every week.

They gave the tickets to Frank and his friends. The Olympia soldiered on until the end of the 1950s. On 7 November 1959, when it was showing *Pirate Submarine* and *Follow That Woman*, the picture house closed. The building is still there on Hyde Road, having gone through many changes. It is currently a furniture store.

Beyond Gorton's shopping centre, towards Manchester, is the three-way junction of Hyde Road, Kirkmanshulme Lane and Mount Road. Close by today lies a housing development called Essoldo Close. The name remembers the picture house which once stood on the site and ended its life as the Essoldo. Gorton's largest picture house, it had opened in 1936 as the Rivoli, under the proprietorship of Ben Kanter. With 1,506 seats it was a great barn of a place, with a stage and eight dressing rooms. At the back of the building were large double doors, through which lighting and scenery were brought in for stage shows.

Frank Rhodes recalls that, as lads in the 1950s, he and his mates would find bits of film at the back of the picture house. Sometimes the film snapped in the projector and the projectionist, to repair it, would have to cut a bit of film off the reel. He threw the cut off pieces of film out

The Rivoli, later Essoldo, Gorton. (Courtesy of Cinema Theatre Association archive)

The Corona, Gorton. (Courtesy of Harry Chamberlain, whose father was manager there for a time)

of the back doors onto the croft behind the picture house, where Frank and his friends found them. Performances at the Rivoli were continuous each evening and seats were modestly priced. The picture house's prime position fostered good business.

Ben Kanter also owned the Rivoli in Collyhurst. In 1946 he sold both picture houses to Sol Sheekman, owner of the Essoldo cinema chain. On becoming part of the Essoldo chain, the picture houses also took its name and the Rivoli Gorton became the Essoldo Gorton. Frank Rhodes recalls:

> The Rivoli sign could still be distinguished behind the new Essoldo sign. The Essoldo was the closest Gorton had to a picture palace. From a spacious foyer there were stairs on either side to a large circle area. The upstairs foyer had settees for patrons to be comfortable while they waited for the usherettes to admit them.

Jean and Derek Wheeldon's memories of the Rivoli/Essoldo were somewhat different: 'It was a very big place, and very cold. You would put your feet up on the back of the seat in front because "things" ran over your feet, and you never knew what they were.' Derek once broke his ankle and had his foot in plaster – only the toes being exposed. He had to keep that foot on the floor and he remembers something running over his toes. The Essoldo continued to do good business for twenty-two years. It showed it last film – *Here We Go Round the Mulberry Bush* – on Saturday, 25 May 1968. It closed that day, and was later used as a bingo hall. The building, on the site until the 1990s, was finally demolished to make way for Essoldo Close.

Gorton, beyond Belle Vue as far as Ardwick, is known as West Gorton and was once home to four picture houses. The area's current cinema, the Showcase multiplex, lies where the old Belle Vue fairground once stood. It has ten cinemas in one building, three more than the whole of Gorton had in cinema's heyday. Birch Street is just below the Showcase complex and runs between Hyde Road and Gorton Lane. The Corona picture house, which opened on Birch Street in 1916, served the local people with film entertainment for forty-two years.

On its opening, the Corona was part of the New Century Cinema Circuit. It was a large building, with seats for 1,100 people. Jean Wheeldon remembers 'a long building, and, if you sat near the back, the screen was the size of postage stamp.' In 1927 the Corona was taken over by Denman/Gaumont and became part of the Gaumont circuit, with which it remained until the Spring of 1950. On 30 April that year, the Corona closed – part of Gaumont's programme to divest itself of cinemas which it considered surplus to requirements. Frank Rhodes remembers the Corona in the 1950s: 'It was up-market, even from the Essoldo. Its exterior was impressive, being white stone with the Corona name in red.'

Every year Kendal and Gents, a Gorton engineering firm, held their Christmas party at the Corona. Frank's next-door neighbour, who worked for the firm, once took Frank to that Christmas party and Frank got a joiner's set as a Christmas present. Although Gaumont closed the Corona, it soon reopened as part of the Snape Circuit, with which it remained for the next eight years. As with many picture houses, though, in the early 1950s the Corona suffered from poor attendances, and a decision was eventually taken that it should close on 4 October 1958. The final programme of films shown there was *Bonjour Tristesse* – an adaptation of the Françoise Sagan novel, starring David Niven and Deborah Kerr – and *Escape from San Quentin*. The building then operated as the Southern Sporting Club for some years. When that closed it was left to rot, before finally being demolished in 1985.

West Gorton's three other picture houses seem to have been bug huts rather than picture palaces. The first of them, the Savoy Picture Palace, was built before the First World War and backed onto Savoy Street, just off Hyde Road – which was probably what gave it its name – but the entrance was on Renshaw Street. Derek Wheeldon remembers 'a very basic place, with wooden benches instead of proper seats and a corrugated iron roof, which made it very noisy when it rained.' It stayed in business, though, until 1948. At that time it closed, the first of the Gorton picture houses to close its doors. It was a closure difficult to understand, since television had not yet begun to make its presence felt in people's homes and there was certainly no shortage of popular stars or big movies.

Along Hyde Road, and across Pottery Lane, Clowes Street is on the right. The New Central Picture Theatre opened here in 1915. It was a small house, and had no balcony, though steps up to the box office at the entrance gave it an impressive frontage. There was another entrance at the side. Jean Wheeldon remembers that, 'when one lot of customers was coming out, some of the lads would walk backwards to try to get in without paying.' The picture house later changed its name to the Central, and then, in 1951, it became the Conway – under which name it operated for the last ten years of its life. It was only when it became the Conway that it began to advertise in the *Manchester Evening News*. The Conway closed on 24 June 1961, after the final showing of *The Rise and Fall of Legs Diamond* and *Born Reckless*, but reopened as the Conway Bingo Club; that too eventually closed. The building remains on Clowes Street, with some kind of commercial use.

Staff of the Corona, Gorton. (Courtesy of Harry Chamberlain)

Saturday morning pictures at the Corona, Gorton. (Courtesy of Harry Chamberlain)

Taylor Street runs from Gorton Lane alongside the recreation ground, and in 1916 a picture house opened at the junction of these roads. Called the King George Picturedrome, probably in honour of the reigning monarch, it was a modest house with just 640 seats. Shows were twice nightly, with matinees three times a week, and seats, at 3*d* and 9*d*, were very moderately priced. In 1929 a change occurred – either a change of name or the building was demolished – and a new picture house took its place. It was known as the Plaza and continued as a picture house into the 1950s. Muriel Longshaw, who was born in 1927 and lived in Gorton for twenty years or so, remembers the Plaza as 'a bug hut, with benches, not seats; it was not a pleasant place.' Her view is echoed by Frank Rhodes, who recalls a 'very dark and dingy place'. In 1957 the Plaza became the second of Gorton's picture houses to close. Unlike many, however, it did not reopen as a bingo hall. For some years the building was used by Smethurst Organ Builders, before finally being demolished.

TEN

OPENSHAW

Ashton Old Road leaves Manchester on its eastern side for the town of Ashton-under-Lyne. In the heyday of the picture house, Openshaw, straddling Ashton Old Road, had no fewer than seven – all on, or near to, a one and a quarter mile stretch of Ashton Old Road, extending from Great Ancoats Street to Fairfield Road. It must have been exciting to walk or ride along Ashton Old Road when all seven cinemas were in business. They would all be lit up, large posters advertising the week's (and possibly the next week's) shows, giving prospective patrons a great choice of film entertainment. Today, with all seven closed and demolished, Ashton Old Road is just a road you drive down to get to Manchester.

Closest to Manchester – between Redvers Street and Baden Street, with its entrance on Ashton Old Road – was the Queen's, opened in 1913. A large building, owned by Bernard Rhodes, it could seat 1,205 people. Performances were continuous each evening, with matinees daily, and the excellent location of the Queen's quickly made it a successful house. In 1932 the Queen's became part of the ABC circuit and remained so till the end of the Second World War, when it reverted to independent status until it joined the Star circuit in 1951. Geoff Logan, who lived in Ardwick for the first thirty years of his life, knew the Queen's: 'I used to go there Saturday afternoons, if I'd been able to take enough empty pop bottles back to the shop to get money for the ticket. It was a nice place, always very clean.'

Harry Shore, now in his seventies, has a rather different memory: 'The Queen's was very run down; you'd only go there if there was something you wanted to see desperately.' Despite the proximity of the other Openshaw houses, not to mention the city centre cinemas, the Queen's kept going until the 1960s, finally ending its life as a picture house on Saturday, 15 April 1961, with a Paramount double bill – Sophia Loren in *It Started in Naples*, supported by *Walk Like a Dragon*. The building became a bingo hall but, when that closed, it was pulled down.

A few yards along Ashton Old Road from the Queen's was the Clock Face hotel, next to which was Royal Street and then the Roy Picturedrome, opened in 1914. The Roy, as it eventually came to be known, was a small house – only 600 seats – and was independently owned. Geoff Logan had a vivid memory of it:

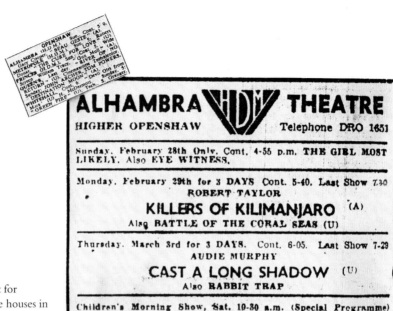

Composite advert for
Openshaw picture houses in
the 1950s.

You went into the Roy by a side door. The front of the place, on Ashton Old Road, was taken up by a butcher's shop, which always had dead things hanging outside. The Roy was a flea pit; it always smelled of carbolic soap.

Harry Shore agrees: 'The Roy was a bug hut. I wouldn't have liked to see it with the lights on.' With fierce competition from the other picture houses along Ashton Old Road, the Roy got by on a programme of reissues and second features which played as main films. Amazingly it managed to stay in business until 1958, though it stopped advertising in the *Manchester Evening News* in 1950 – perhaps indicating that business was not good. Joyce Rogers recalls that, 'the Roy was a very small place. But we would go there because it would let in under-age teenagers to see X certificate films, which you had to be eighteen to see usually.' After closure the Roy was eventually demolished.

Openshaw was unusual in the Manchester area in having not one, but two, major theatres in the early years of the twentieth century. The first one, the Metropole Theatre, opened in 1898 on Ashton Old Road. In 1907 it was taken over by W.H. Broadhead. With seating for nearly 2,000 people it was a huge place, used for straight plays, variety shows and, from 1909, for silent pictures too. It often had animal acts and circuses at Christmas and in the summer. Joyce Rogers remembers: 'One year they put a circus on at the Metropole and an elephant walked up Ashton Old Road with its trainer, followed by lorries carrying other animals in cages.'

As films began to take over from live theatre as the most popular entertainment, the owners of the Metropole realised that films were more profitable than stage shows. In the 1930s the Metropole became a picture house, becoming part of the HDM circuit in 1938. Harry Shore remembers a very impressive place, one of the last picture houses to have a commissionaire, who would walk along the queue shouting 'Two seats in the rear stalls!' He recalls: 'When it became a cinema they kept "the gods" open. You went into them from the back of the place

The Queen's picture house, Ashton Old Road. (Courtesy of Manchester Archives and Local Studies, Central Library)

The Theatre Metropole, Ashton Old Road, in the 1930s before it was converted to a cinema.

and sat on wooden benches.' Joyce Rogers adds: 'There were two boxes in the circle, either side of the stage. I imagine that people who sat there when it was a cinema got stiff necks from looking at the screen sideways.'

The Metropole did well with films and prospered for some years. At the Saturday matinee it had a talent contest for the children. The prize, Joyce recalls, was a bag of sweets. Because the Metropole was a large house it would have been difficult to fill, especially when audiences started to decline in the 1950s. It ended its life as a picture house on Saturday, 21 March 1959. The final films shown there were *These Dangerous Years*, starring pop singer Frankie Vaughan, and *Dig That Uranium*. The building remained for some years but was demolished when the area was redeveloped.

Bosworth Street, which ran behind the Metropole, joined Grey Mare Lane. A picture house opened on Grey Mare Lane, just before its junction with Bosworth Street, in 1915. The newcomer was called King George's Picture Theatre. It was a large house with seats for 1,600 people. Harry Shore lived in Bosworth Street as a boy, and his bedroom looked out onto the back of the picture house which, in 1930, became the Prince's Picture Theatre. Harry describes the Prince's thus:

> It was a nice place. You entered from a side passage and the seats at the front were wooden forms, not proper seats. There was once a fire at the Prince's in the middle of the night. My bedroom overlooked the place but I slept right through all the excitement.

The Prince's prospered through the boom years of the 1930s and 1940s; then, as with most other picture houses, attendances began to fall in the 1950s. For some time the Prince's, like several other Openshaw houses, was part of the HDM circuit, but inevitably it succumbed to 'progress' and finally closed its doors as a picture house on Saturday, 28 October 1961. Its final programme was two Walt Disney pictures, *The Absent-minded Professor* and *The Horsemasters*. The building reopened and operated for some time as a nightclub, the Domino Club, but eventually that closed and the building was demolished.

Harry Shore lived with his mother and grandmother – who were keen on the pictures – in Bosworth Street, within running distance of the Queen's, the Roy, the Metropole and the

Sheila Fitzpatrick (far right) with friends at the Domino Club, former Prince's picture house, 1963.

A painting (originally in colour) of the refurbished
Prince's picture house, by Harry Shore.

Prince's. Harry remembers often being urged to 'Run along the road, son, and see which one has
the longest queue,' so that his mother and grandmother could decide which cinema to patronise.

Ashton Old Road runs into Higher Openshaw, with a slight incline; shortly before that, also
on the left, it once passed Openshaw Picture Hall – which the Openshaw Picture Hall Co. Ltd
manager, W.E. Egerton, opened in the early years of the twentieth century. It could seat 830
people and eventually its name was changed to the Rex. Sonia Jones, *née* Brodrick, was born
and brought up in Openshaw and remembers the Rex: 'I didn't go there often. It was a bug hut.
If you went there, you'd come out scratching.'

Like the Roy, the Rex existed mainly on B movies and films that had played one or other
of the Openshaw cinemas months earlier. Harry Shore recalls that this had its advantages:
'It was a run down place and it showed mainly pictures that had been around for months.
It gave you the chance to see pictures which you missed first time around and were keen to see.'
For a time in the 1930s, the Rex, like several other Openshaw houses, was part of the HDM
circuit. It ceased to advertise in the *Manchester Evening News* in the 1950s, and later in that
decade finally closed and was demolished.

In the centre of Higher Openshaw, Ashton Old Road meets Old Lane, just before the junction
with Fairfield Street. Openshaw's two remaining picture houses stood near the junction, one just
on Old Lane, the other on Ashton Old Road. The smaller of the two, on Old Lane, was the
Whitehall Picture Palace, opened in 1915 by the Whitehall Cinema Co. Ltd. The Whitehall, as
it was commonly known, had 800 seats and, in its early days, there were two performances each
evening, prices ranging from 4*d* to 1*s*. Despite having a competitor just yards away, around the
corner on Ashton Old Road, the Whitehall did good business for forty years or so. It was always
an independently owned picture place and people have good memories of it.

David Milner grew up in Openshaw in the 1950s and 1960s. He liked going to the Whitehall
best 'because, when you came out late evening, the chippy was still open and you could buy 4*d*
worth of chips and walk home instead of getting the bus.' David also recalls:

I always found the Whitehall intimidating, as did most kids who went there. The one-armed
fireman who was on duty most nights, and was in charge of the gas lights that were placed along

the walls, patrolled the place. One word from him and dozens of kids would quickly make sure that their feet, which had been resting on the back of the seat in front, immediately hit the floor.

Sonia Jones, *née* Brodrick, got into the Whitehall free because her dad was the manager, and remembers that 'the front entrance of the Whitehall faced Openshaw's sweet shop, which did very well from people who were spending the night at the pictures.' In 1957, the owners decided to refurbish the Whitehall. It closed on 6 May 1957 'for extensive alterations'. These were unveiled a month later on 10 June 1957, along with a new name – the Regal – and a huge box office hit. The adverts described it as 'Openshaw's luxury cinema', a fitting setting for the musical *High Society*. Prices were 1s in the front stalls, 1s 6d in the rear stalls and 2s in the circle. The Regal opened to good business.

Though new, it was by no means exempt from the haemorrhaging of audiences which was affecting picture houses in those years, staying open for just under seven years, until Saturday, 15 February 1964. By coincidence Frank Sinatra, one of whose biggest hits had opened it, was also in the closing film, the comedy *Come Blow Your Horn*, which was supported by *The Painted Smile*. The building operated as a bingo hall until 1980 and then became a warehouse. In 1990 the upper storey was demolished. In 2008 the old picture house had been reduced to a shop selling second-hand electrical goods, and, early in 2009, the building was finally demolished.

The last of Openshaw's picture houses was the Alhambra Theatre, which opened in 1908 on Ashton Old Road, just round the corner from where the Whitehall later stood. The Alhambra started to show films in 1914 and, in 1928, H.D. Moorhouse – who had been managing director

of Alhambra (M/C) Ltd, the theatre's owners – bought the theatre and made it the first in his HDM circuit. The original theatre seating (2,000) was reduced to 1,572, still a large house. As a girl, Sonia Jones lived a stone's throw from the Alhambra, and often went there: 'It was a lovely place. Chic Hibbert's dance hall was above the cinema; you entered it from the side street, not through the picture house.'

The Alhambra cinema retained the theatre's stage and dressing rooms but operated as a picture house for almost fifty years. Betty Bamber, brought up in Openshaw, recalls: 'An early memory was going to the cinema in the war. My elder sister took me in the blackout, no street lights, such an adventure.' This author, coming to the North West to work in 1959, remembers the 219 bus – from

The Alhambra Theatre, Ashton Old Road, before it was converted to a cinema.

Manchester to Ashton – stopped outside the Alhambra, which was showing *The Big Circus* and *King of the Wild Stallions*. A few months later, on 6 April 1960, the Alhambra's final films were *This Other Eden* and a Danny Kaye oldie *Up in Arms*. The stage and dressing rooms were demolished, the auditorium was gutted, and the building was turned into the Alhambra Restaurant – which closed in 2007. The building has since been demolished.

CINEMA MANAGER – JACK OF ALL TRADES

The Brodrick family – father, mother, three daughters and one son – lived in Rosina Street, Openshaw. Dad Michael, after military service in the First World War, returned to Openshaw. To support his family he took the job of manager at the Whitehall cinema.

The staff of Whitehall consisted of the manager, the projectionist, a lady called Florence Morgan who worked in the pay box, an usherette and a fire officer. Michael, as manager, was in front of house when the cinema opened each day. He put up the posters for the week's attractions, taking his bucket of paste, a brush and the posters and pasting up Monday, Tuesday and Wednesday's films on one side of the front entrance; Thursday, Friday and Saturday's on the other. He used to pedal down to Manchester on his bicycle to pick up the films for programme changes, and his daughter Audrey, would urge him, 'There's a new picture that looks really good Dad. Please get it.' Michael, who also had to control the yelling kids at the Saturday morning matinees, remained manager of the Whitehall until the outbreak of the Second World War, when he was called up for more important war work.

Michael Brodrick who, for some years after the First World War, managed the Whitehall picture house in Openshaw.

ELEVEN

MANCHESTER CITY CENTRE

Manchester city centre had plenty to offer in film entertainment. Several picture houses showing silent films did not survive for very long, but, in the centre of the city, a dozen houses had long and lucrative lifetimes. For many years, from Peter Street, along Oxford Street and Oxford Road, picture-goers were able to choose their films from no fewer than nine picture houses.

The oldest picture house, excluding those which had originally been theatres, opened in 1911 on Oxford Street, under the ownership of Provincial Cinematic Theatres Ltd. The Picture House was opened by the Lord Mayor of Manchester; its first programme included pictures of Captain Scott's expedition to the South Pole; proceeds were in aid of the Manchester Geographical Society's fund for the expedition. Performances were continuous from 2 p.m. and seats were priced at 6d and 1s, with children admitted for half price before 5 p.m. The cinema seated 1,100 people and, from its location on Oxford Road, soon became known as the Oxford Picture House. When the Market Street Picture House opened in 1916, the two, owned by the same company, shared the same programme. The Oxford Picture House, which became the Oxford Theatre in April 1927, and the New Oxford Theatre in August of the same year, was the first Manchester house to show a talkie – Universal's *Uncle Tom's Cabin*, which was, in fact, only part talkie, since it had been shot as a silent, with sound effects and music added before it was released.

The New Oxford thrived into the 1940s, changing hands several times and finally becoming part of the Buxton Theatre Circuit in 1949. When widescreen films, in the shape of CinemaScope, were introduced in 1953, the New Oxford quickly adapted for them, and showed the western, *The Command*, in August 1954. Then, when Twentieth Century Fox fell out with the Rank organisation (whose Odeon and Gaumont cinemas usually showed Fox pictures), the New Oxford, with the Deansgate cinema, became Fox's showplace in Manchester, showing films like *Demetrius and the Gladiators* and the *Egyptian*. Its enterprising owners, conscious of the fact that ABC had no central Manchester house, also played *Gigi*, the Oscar winning musical, for nine months, and *The Nun's Story* for four months in 1959-'60.

In June 1960, the Rank organisation took over the New Oxford, giving it three cinemas within a hundred yards on Oxford Street. The author was in the audience one Saturday in September 1960 to see Alfred Hitchcock's *Psycho*. When the private detective was attacked by a

Composite advert for Manchester city centre cinemas in the early 1940s. Note that the Oxford and Market Street picture houses share the same film.

figure which rushed out of the bedroom, in one of the film's most gruesome scenes, the author jumped, and the fellow sitting next to him yelled, 'For God's sake mate, you frightened the s★★★ out of me!'

Rank operated the New Oxford for the rest of its life, showcasing some important pictures, including *Ben-Hur*. Rank, though, never regarded the New Oxford as the equal of its Odeon and Gaumont neighbours, and, after the destruction of the Gaumont and the twinning of the Odeon, Rank programmed the New Oxford with films which were more suited to small houses, making the picture house unviable. Rank finally closed it on 25 October 1980, the last film being Walter Hill's *The Long Riders*. The building remains on Oxford Street today, a MacDonald's occupying part of the frontage. The name, the Oxford Picture House, is still clearly visible on a plaque above the entrance.

Market Street has always been one of Manchester's busiest shopping streets – though never an entertainment venue, boasting just one picture house, and, since 1974, not even one. The Market Street Picture House opened in 1914, on a corner facing Spring Gardens, its entrance looking down Market Street. Owned, like the Oxford, by Provincial Cinematograph Theatres Ltd, this was a small house, seating 600 people. Sound came to the Market Street house in January 1930, and business was good through the 1930s and during the Second World War. The location was something of a disadvantage in the 1940s, since it was the Oxford Street area that usually attracted people looking to see a film, and in the late 1940s business fell away.

This persuaded the management to change the name in September 1949 to the Market Street News Theatre, showing travel films in colour, cartoons and newsreels. That lasted just six months, closing in February 1950.

The picture house reopened five days later as the Continental, committed to showing the best of European cinema. French actress Anouk Aimée, star of the first film *Les Amants de Vérone*, attended the opening. Over the next two and a half years, the Continental showed the best of European cinema, with stars like Anna Magnani and Fernandel. Mancunians, however, failed to support the picture house and it closed in June 1952, reopening as a news theatre. This time it lasted for eight months, closing again in February 1953, to reopen the next day under its original name, the Market Street Cinema, still showing European productions. The owners struggled along for just over two years before closing the picture house again. At that point Jacey Cinemas took the house over and renamed it the Cinephone.

For a while the Cinephone showed the best of European films. However, when the author came to Manchester in 1959 it was getting by on European sex movies with lurid titles like *The Lustful Vicar* and *Seduced in Sodom*. Margaret Back worked at the Cinephone as an usherette for two years at the end of the 1950s:

> The manager was Mr Twells. Because of the content of the films we nicknamed the place 'The Sinpit'. We sometimes had to patrol the aisles to keep an eye on dubious members of the audience. Not all the films were of a salacious nature. The Cinephone did show *Richard III* and *Ivan the Terrible*.

The New Oxford cinema, 1960. (Courtesy of Cinema Theatre Association archive)

Staff of the Cinephone (previously Market Street Picture House) at ABC cinemas Christmas dance, *c.* 1960.

By that time, however, it was a rather seedy, run down place, and it was several years before the author visited it. For some unfathomable reason an American picture called *Borderlines*, starring the great Joan Crawford, was showing. I had no intention of missing a Crawford picture, so I went on Saturday afternoon, worried about being seen going in and who the other patrons might be. I needn't have worried – I was the only one in the place, and enjoyed the picture very much.

The Cinephone miraculously stayed in business until 1974. Then the decision was taken to redevelop the area behind Market Street and the Cinephone was subject to a compulsory purchase order. It closed on Monday, 14 January 1974, beaten not by lack of audiences, but by the developers. The final programme? *The Queer, The Erotic* and *Where Are You Going All Naked?*, described by the management as a 'special' farewell programme. And in Cinephone's place? The monstrous Arndale Centre!

There was a picture house at the cathedral end of Deansgate, one of Manchester's main shopping streets, before the First World War. On 21 February 1916 a new, purpose-built picture house, the Deansgate Picture House And Café Rendezvous opened there – capitalising on the weather: 'Delightfully warm in the coldest weather,' said the adverts.

The cinema, with 870 seats, operated on a continuous performance basis, from 12 noon to 10.30 p.m. Stalls seats cost 6d and balcony seats 1s. The cinema quickly became a popular venue, operating as a home of silent pictures for fourteen years, strangely being slower to adopt sound than most other city centre houses. A change of ownership in 1930 led to the installation of a Western Electric sound system and the Deansgate's first sound films were *The Office Wife* and *Those Who Dance* – two Warner Brothers' pictures.

The Deansgate continued through the war years as a popular central Manchester venue, with several changes of ownership; for a time it was part of the HDM circuit. In the early 1950s it was owned by Brennan's Cinemas Ltd, with seat prices from 2s 9d to 3s 6d. One of the most popular pictures shown at the Deansgate was David Lean's film of Harold Brighouse's play *Hobson's Choice*, starring Charles Laughton, John Mills and the excellent Brenda De Banzie. It ran for seven weeks at the Deansgate in 1954 – the kind of run which usually only occurred in London's West End.

In the mid-1950s the Deansgate became, with the Oxford, the Manchester home of Twentieth Century Fox CinemaScope pictures, after Fox fell out with the Rank Organisation (owners of the Odeon and Gaumont circuits). Fox's third CinemaScope picture, *Beneath the 12-Mile Reef*, played the Deansgate. The author's first visit to the Deansgate was in early 1960, to see a glossy melodrama called *The Best of Everything*, which boasted in its cast the legendary Joan Crawford. By that time the Deansgate was a rather scruffy place, with a floor which sloped rather steeply down from the rear stalls to the screen. Another change in the Deansgate's fortunes took place in 1960, when James Brennan Ltd sold the house to the ABC chain, which had long wanted a venue in central Manchester.

The Deansgate closed in May 1960 for alterations, redecoration and the installation of a 70mm screen, reopening in early September as the ABC Deansgate, with a Todd-AO version of *Oklahoma*. Although the film had been shown in Manchester five years earlier, its Deansgate showing was a great success, lasting for five months. The refurbished cinema, which now gave patrons the chance to see films in very luxurious surroundings, was a distinct improvement from the scruffy Deansgate of the 1950s. The ABC Deansgate played some very big movies through the 1960s, including Nicholas Ray's fine epic on the life of Christ, *King of Kings*, and David Lean's *Dr Zhivago*. It also showed a 70mm revival of *Gone with the Wind* – a disaster, which cut off the tops of the characters' heads and their feet in close-up.

In the 1970s the ABC Deansgate became the only Manchester cinema to be equipped to show Sensurround, when it screened *Earthquake*, whose sound effects made the cinema seem to shake when the earthquake happened. Another first for the ABC Deansgate came in early 1971, when it became the first cinema in Manchester city centre to be twinned. The Regal Studios on Oxford Road had been opened in the 1930s as a twin cinema. The new ABC Deansgate 2 opened with Bryan Forbes' film *The Raging Moon*, and Forbes and his wife – actress Nanette Newman, who starred in the film – were in attendance. The ABC chain was owned by Thorn-EMI, which operated the cinemas until 1986 when it sold the chain to Cannon. Cannon operated the Deansgate twins until 1990, when, as they had done with many other houses, they suddenly announced that the Deansgate cinemas were to close. They did, on Thursday, 9 August 1990, when Cannon 1 was showing *Gremlins 2: The New Batch*, and the smaller Cannon 2 was continuing the run of *Back to the Future III*, which had started in Cannon 1. The cinema building still stands on Deansgate, today operating as a pub, the Moon Under Water.

At the beginning of the twentieth century, the Mosley hotel stood between Tib Street and Oldham Street, facing Piccadilly Gardens. It closed in the early 1920s and the building was bought by Piccadilly Picture Theatre (Manchester) Ltd, which opened the Piccadilly Picture Theatre in the building in the summer of 1922. This would prove to be the shortest lived of all the Manchester houses, lasting a mere fifteen years. On its opening, however, it was a very popular place – a good location, the inclusion of a dance-hall (in the basement), a café, and a restaurant making it a favourite venue for a night out.

The first film to be shown at the Piccadilly Picture Theatre was an adaptation of Dickens' *The Old Curiosity Shop* and managing director Charles Ogden brought the venue a great coup when, in 1927, it played MGM's silent version of *Ben-Hur* starring Ramon Novarro. It showed four times a day with an orchestral accompaniment. The management of the Piccadilly Picture Theatre showed commendable foresight in cooperating with some of the early experiments in sound films; though, when they showed their first talkie, *Weary River*, starring Richard Barthelmess, the adverts seemed to acknowledge that – with sound films already being shown at the Oxford and the Theatre Royal – they had missed the boat: 'You will soon listen while you look, Piccadilly. He who talks last, talks best.'

The Piccadilly continued into the 1930s, claiming that it was 'the house of consistency', and then, in the week of 2 August 1937, the management announced that it was to close. No reason was given, but the signature of T.E. Robinson (liquidator) among those signing the closure notice suggests that the reason was financial. That week the film showing was, ironically, *The Show Goes On*, starring Gracie Fields. Gracie, appearing that summer at the Grand Theatre Blackpool, spoke to the Piccadilly Picture Theatre's audience that closing night. The final cinema ticket was allocated to a Stretford woman, the picture house's first patron on its opening day. The building remains in Piccadilly today – much altered and now housing, on the ground floor, a branch of Boots the Chemist.

Theatres often changed to picture houses when film became the cheapest, most accessible form of entertainment in the early twentieth century. Manchester had had a Theatre Royal since 1775, first in Spring Gardens and then in Fountain Street – both of which were destroyed by fire. In 1844 the owner, John Knowles, decided to build a new Theatre Royal on Peter Street. It opened on 29 September 1845 and provided theatrical entertainment until 1921, when it became the property of Bernard Pollock. Concerned at falling attendances – caused by the increasing number of city centre theatres and by the popularity of the new picture houses – he decided to show films at the Theatre Royal. Alterations took place, including the removal of the theatre's four balconies, and the Theatre Royal opened as a picture house on 4 September 1922 with the British film *The Game of Life*.

Because it was intended that the building should still be able to stage live shows, the Theatre Royal retained two orchestras. Among its earliest successes in silent pictures, though with a live prologue and epilogue, was Rudolph Valentino in *The Four Horsemen of the Apocalypse*. The Theatre Royal became Manchester's second picture house, after the Oxford, to adapt for sound. In January 1929 it showed its first talkie, the Oscar-winning *Wings*, which was soon followed by Warner Baxter winning the Best Actor Oscar in *In Old Arizona*.

The Theatre Royal also had a big success with Paramount's 'thrilling, all-talking production' *The Dummy*! The picture house continued to be successful into the 1950s, with various changes of management. In the early 1930s it was part of the ABC circuit; from 1935 to 1937 the owners were Garrett Klement Theatres Ltd, and from 1937 to the end of the war it was part of the HDM circuit. A false front, put on the building in the Garrett Klement era, was blown off by a bomb during the war. As audiences declined in the 1950s, the Theatre Royal, being an independent picture house, saw takings plummet. When 3D films became the rage in 1953 it jumped aboard that bandwagon, and enjoyed full houses with films like *House of Wax* and *Kiss Me Kate*, but 3D pictures never really caught on.

As an independent cinema, the Theatre Royal did not have access to the big Hollywood movies from Twentieth Century Fox, Universal and Paramount – which went to Rank, or MGM and Warner Brothers, which played the ABC circuit. By the early 1960s the management, City Cinemas (Manchester), was running out of ideas. Then, in a great piece of showmanship, they took a gamble. Cinerama, with its huge screen, had been a money-spinning hit in London since the early 1950s. When MGM/Cinerama made *How the West Was Won* in 1962, quickly followed by *The Wonderful World of the Brothers Grimm*, the management of the Theatre Royal took the decision to bring Cinerama to Manchester. The Theatre Royal closed in September 1963; a huge new screen, 65ft by 28ft, was installed, seating was reduced from 1,800 to 1,000 and *How the West Was Won* in Cinerama had its gala premiere on Monday, 4 November 1963. It ran for seven months, attracting audiences from all over the North West as well as further afield, and gave the Theatre Royal a new lease of life. Not for long however! Cinerama product became harder to obtain, and the Theatre Royal had to show smaller, less profitable films, so that by the late 1960s there was talk of demolishing it to build an office block. It soldiered on until August 1972, when it closed on Sunday 13 August after the final showing, on the vast Cinerama screen, of Rodgers and Hammerstein's *The King and I*. Since then the building has been used for bingo and a disco. In mid 2010, however, it will become the new home of Manchester's Library Theatre – welcome news indeed.

Across the street from the Theatre Royal, on the site of a former circus, the Gaiety Theatre of Varieties (built in 1878) burned down six years later. Its replacement, the Comedy Theatre, functioned on the site until 1903. The United Theatres Co. reopened it and ran it until

The former Theatre Royal cinema as a nightclub at the end of the twentieth century.

1907, when they sold the building to Miss Horniman. Theatre continued there until 1920, when Miss Horniman sold the premises to Abe Hollander, managing director of the Futurist Picture House lower down Peter Street. He, seeing a more profitable future in films than in theatre, reopened the building as the Gaiety Picture House on 18 July 1921. The event was graced by the presence of actress Ellen Terry, then celebrating her sixty-fifth anniversary as an actress.

The Gaiety's first film was *The Luck of Geraldine Laird*, starring Bessie Barriscale, and it was an instant success as a picture house. One of its biggest silent movie hits was Douglas Fairbanks' version of *The Black Pirate*, 'seen by 6,000 people and missed by a disappointed 4,000', according to the management. At Christmas 1929 the Gaiety featured MGM's first talkie, *White Shadows of the South Seas*, when the MGM lion was heard roaring for the first time.

Briefly part of the ABC circuit in the early 1930s, the Gaiety frequently showed the same programme as the Deansgate. The 1,434-seat Gaiety continued as a picture house until the Christmas of 1937, when the pantomime *Dick Whittington* played there. Afterwards it reverted to theatrical shows; but, after being closed for six months from the summer of 1939, it reopened as a picture house on 26 February 1940 with the hit *The Real Glory*, starring Gary Cooper.

The building operated as a picture house and variety hall for the next few years and, in May 1940, had the Manchester showing of David Selznick's masterpiece *Gone with the Wind*, which ran for an astonishing twenty-two weeks. Other big hits for the Gaiety in the early 1940s were Charlie Chaplin's *The Great Dictator* and the Spencer Tracy, Ingrid Bergman, Lana Turner version of *Dr Jekyll and Mr Hyde* – both for six-week runs.

The BBC wanted to buy the Gaiety in 1941 as a home for the BBC Repertory Company, but the building continued as a picture house through the 1940s, attracting good audiences. In 1948 the local watch committee forced the Gaiety to close for alterations. The theatre had its stalls area below ground level and its projection box at ground floor level. Because of the risk of fire, the watch committee wanted the projection box moved to balcony level and the gallery seats to be removed. The management had to comply in order to continue in business, so the Gaiety closed for four months in 1948 so that the work could be carried out. The Gaiety suffered from all the faults of a converted theatre – the circle was too steep and the pillars which supported it were always in your way if you sat in the stalls.

It remained a popular venue, although the big pictures from the major studios were often denied it, meaning that the big stars of the 1950s – Gregory Peck, Robert Mitchum, Doris Day and Susan Hayward – were rarely seen on its screen. It had notable success, though, with films like the technicolored *The Naked Jungle*, and the horror movie *Them*. In 1959, however, the owners sold the building and it closed on 1 August that year. The final film was the gangster picture *Al Capone*, starring Rod Steiger. Workmen moved in soon afterwards and stripped the interior; within days the building, which had stood on the site for more than seventy years, had vanished. Just two plaques were left on the wall of Television House to show that a theatre had once stood there.

The coming of sound led to an increasing number of picture houses being built. Three new ones opened on Oxford Street/Oxford Road within two weeks of each other in the autumn of 1930. Through the summer, adverts in the Manchester press were heralding the opening of a brand new film venue in the city centre, calling the cinema 'Two cosy theatres in one' and 'sound in construction for sound reproduction'.

The Regal Twins – for they were in fact two picture houses in one – opened on Saturday, 20 September 1930. They were on the second floor of the building, reached by stairs or a lift, and each had its own separate foyer. They were built back-to-back, with the projection box in the centre so that one screen was at the All Saints end of the auditorium, the other at the Oxford Street end. Each of them could seat 800 patrons and it was the intention that one should have continuous performances, the other, if necessary, separate performances. Seats were bookable and there was a car park. The management – Piccadilly Picture Theatre (Manchester) – was careful to stress that each picture house would have its own programme and, for the opening week, the Number 1 Theatre had a film called *Vengeance* and the Number 2 Theatre a Fox musical called *High Society Blues*, starring the popular team Charles Farrell and Janet Gaynor.

The new cinemas, with their luxurious ambience and comfortable seating, were an instant hit, doing good business through the 1930s and the war years. By the beginning of the 1940s both usually showed the same programme. They were also mainly second-run houses, showing films which had already been shown at the Paramount, Gaumont and other city centre venues. This continued throughout the 1940s and 1950s, with films like *The Third Man* playing with great success.

Whereas circuit cinemas kept films just one week, the Regal Twins played popular pictures for extended runs. CinemaScope came to the Regal with the Roman epic *Sign of the Pagan* in February 1955. The Regal often showed the same programme as the Ardwick Apollo. Marjorie Jackson has a vivid memory of a most embarrassing moment at the Regal:

I was on a first date with a boy, who took me to the Regal. We sat down to watch the film and I fell asleep. I only woke when the boy I was with woke me up. I had slept through the whole film.

The Regal changed hands in 1960 when it was bought by the Leeds-based Star Cinemas; it closed for a month while the foyers and auditoria were redecorated, and the front of the house completely altered with a new V-shaped canopy to carry details of the week's programmes. The cinemas were renamed the Romulus and the Remus – after the twins of Roman legend – and a replica of the statue of the twins being suckled by the she-wolf stood near the box office. They also became first-run cinemas, reopening with the popular *Three Worlds of Gulliver* and an Audie Murphy western *Seven Ways from Sundown*.

In the summer of 1962 the cinemas were renamed Studio 1 and Studio 2, and they began to show completely different programmes, beginning with *The Webster Boy* in Studio 1 and *The Wooden Horse of Troy* in Studio 2. Late in the 1960s a Gala Film Club, strictly for members only, began operating in one of the cinemas, showing films which were denied to the general public. The owners, not content with two cinemas in one building, decided there was room for more, so Studio 1 closed for a month in early 1972 for conversion to a four-screen cinema.

The new studios, advertised as 'Europe's first 5 cinema centre' opened for business on 30 March 1972 as Studios 1 to 5. Studio 1 had *Steptoe and Son*, Studio 2 *Klute*, Studio 3 *What Are You Doing After the Orgy?*, Studio 4 *Play Misty for Me* and Studio 5 Chaplin's *Modern Times*. Star Cinemas continued to operate the five-screen complex, adding four more screens on Deansgate – Studios 6 to 9 – in December 1972. In 1985, however, the Cannon Group, aggressively expanding its interests in Britain, bought out Star Cinemas, taking control of all its houses, including the five screens of the old Regal.

Former Regal building, now home of Dancehouse Theatre.

A year later, in August 1985, when Cannon also gained control of the Deansgate twin cinemas, it decided abruptly to close Studios 1 to 5. That happened after the final showings on Thursday, 25 September 1986. Studio 1 was showing *Poltergeist 2*, Studio 2 *The Karate Kid* Studio 3 *Pretty in Pink*, Studio 4 *Rebel* and Studio 5 the soft porn programme *Erotic Eva*, *Confessions of a Male Escort* and *Confessions of a Sexy Photographer*. Cannon could truly be dubbed 'The death knell of picture houses', its closures being much more numerous than its openings. In 1999, the building which had housed the Regal – derelict for some years – was finally taken over and converted to today's Dancehouse Theatre. One is grateful that, today, when old picture houses are supermarkets, funeral directors' premises or, horror of horrors, car parks, this building is still used for entertainment.

PAGE BOY AT THE REGAL

Harry Edwards, born in 1929, had his first job at the Regal:

> At fourteen I became a pageboy at the Regal Twins. The long hours started at 10 a.m. My first task was to vacuum the large carpeted foyer and polish the many brass handles of the entrance doors. Doors opened at about 11 a.m. That was when I put on my multi-buttoned green uniform and shell jacket, and operated the lift up to the cinemas, which were on the second floor. The cinema was never empty during the war years; service men and women of all nationalities were everywhere: Poles, Australians, Free French, and American sailors. The queue for admittance often circled the block. One young man who worked in the projection box was called up, went over to France and soon afterwards he was killed. The management had a commemorative plaque made – to Private Bernard Keenan – and mounted it on the wall in the entrance foyer. My working day ended at the end of the last screening, about 11 p.m. I had two one-hour breaks during the day and earned the princely sum of £4 5s 11d after stoppages.

Two weeks after the Regal opened for business, another brand new cinema – this one a veritable picture palace – opened its doors some 300 yards away, back towards the city centre. Described by the *Manchester Evening News* as 'Manchester's slice of the Great White Way', the newcomer, belonging to the US studio Paramount, bore the studio's name, the Paramount. Designed by Frank Thomas Verity F.R.I.B.A and his associate Samuel Beverley – who had designed the Plaza and the Carlton in London's West End – the Paramount could seat 1,400 patrons in the stalls, 650 in the mezzanine and 950 in the grand circle. All seats cost 1s between noon and 1 p.m. (except the mezzanine); between 1 p.m. and 4 p.m. the stalls cost 1s 6d, the grand circle and balcony 1s, and the mezzanine 2s 4d. Evening prices were: balcony 1s 3d, stalls 1s 6d and 2s 4d, grand circle 2s, and mezzanine 2s 4d and 3s 6d.

The Paramount's first manager was Mr C. Young. The first film shown there was the musical *The Love Parade*, starring Maurice Chevalier and – her film debut – Jeanette MacDonald, and

Three momentous events in Manchester cinema – the coming of sound, the introduction of CinemaScope and the premiere of Cinerama.

featuring the hit song 'Dream Lover'. The Paramount could also stage spectacular variety shows, and was an instant hit with the Manchester public. It showed the first films made in Technicolor, a documentary about Bali called *Lelong* and the first full-length Technicolor feature, Rouben Mamoulian's film *Becky Sharp*. The Paramount always got the pick of the new pictures, including, soon after the outbreak of war, *Beau Geste*, starring Gary Cooper, Ray Milland and Robert Preston.

Manchester people were puzzled in early 1940 by adverts in the press proclaiming 'Get used to saying Odeon'. All became clear in April of that year when the Paramount changed its name to Odeon; Paramount had sold several of its UK picture houses to the Odeon circuit. The Odeon – through the 1940s and into the 1950s one of Manchester's premier cinemas – was chosen in 1954 to be adapted for the first production filmed in CinemaScope, *The Robe*. This ran for four weeks, although the Odeon usually kept films for only one week.

Odeon staff, 1957. Current manager, Mr Beaumont, is centre, front row.

The Odeon as a seven-screen multiplex, 1998.

The Gaumont, Oxford Street. The New Oxford was just beyond it and the Odeon a little further towards the Central Library, on the opposite side of the street.

The author's first visit to the Odeon was for Robert Wise's powerful anti-capital punishment picture *I Want to Live*, featuring Susan Hayward's brilliant Oscar-winning portrayal of Barbara Graham. The Odeon then played the Rank circuit's main releases, while the Gaumont had extended runs for 70mm pictures. Nevertheless, the Odeon flourished with Doris Day comedies, the Bond movies and Marilyn Monroe's last three pictures, *Some Like it Hot*, *The Misfits* and *Let's Make Love*. Sometimes, however, the Odeon showcased a brilliant film better suited to a smaller venue. One such was 1967's *The Whisperers*, in which the magnificent Edith Evans gave one of cinema's truly great performances as a lonely old lady. The performance deserved full houses; this author saw it in the vast Odeon, which was almost empty. Stage performance often featured at the Odeon on Sunday evenings, and among those who played there were Johnny Mathis, Tom Jones and the Beach Boys.

When, in the early 1970s, it became the practice to twin and triple cinemas, Rank decided that the Odeon was their most suitable house for twinning in Manchester, closing it in July 1973 for almost six months. The twinning involved retaining the stalls as one cinema, and dropping a wall down from the ceiling of the building to the front of the circle to make the other. The mezzanine was not used. The two new cinemas opened with a gala charity premiere in January 1974, Odeon 1 showing Nicolas Roeg's adaptation of a Daphne Du Maurier story *Don't Look Now* and Odeon 2 *Carry on Girls*. Although the new cinemas were successful, their creation and Rank's ruthless handling of their two other Oxford Street houses – the Gaumont and the New Oxford – decimated opportunities for picture-going in what had, for some forty years, been a Mecca for filmgoers in Manchester.

In 1979 Rank added a third cinema, Odeon 3, to the complex, utilising what had been the mezzanine; that one opened with *Love at First Bite*, a Dracula spoof. Then, in 1992, came four new screens. The Mezzanine cinema became Odeon 5. The rear of the stalls was converted to two cinemas, Odeon 3 and Odeon 6, with a common projection room. The stage area – behind the screen in Odeon 2 – became Odeon 4 and Odeon 7 was built in the basement. Only Odeon 1 survived intact from the twinning of the early 1970s. The changes wrought in the Odeon by Rank, to make it a venue able to compete with the new multiplexes, can be described as vandalism. The beautiful picture palace that was the Paramount, with its staircase and its beautiful plaster work, was torn apart in the name of profit.

The seven-screen Odeon was not the place to see pictures and Manchester folk soon showed that they knew that. In September 2004, faced with falling attendances, and competition from the AMC multiplex just down the road, and the Printworks multiplex across the city, the Odeon closed. The building still remains on Oxford Street, boarded up and falling deeper into decay. Appeals to the city council to save it for community use, and to English Heritage to give it listed building status, have fallen on deaf ears. So a historic building, a vital part of entertaining Mancunians for some seventy years, is probably destined to become an unnecessary office block, a shopping mall or – like its sister cinema, the Gaumont – a car park.

USHERETTE AT THE ODEON

Anne Schafer has lived for many years in the United States; with her friend, Margaret Back, she was once an usherette at the Odeon:

I was working in an office and decided an evening job would help out at home. The assistant manager at the Odeon interviewed and appointed me, telling me to wear light make-up, flat shoes and always be on time. My office job finished at 5.30 p.m. and I would fly down Oxford Street to be on time for parade in the mezzanine foyer at the Odeon. The staff lined up in the mezzanine and were inspected by the supervisor, Miss Maureen McCormick, who let us know in no uncertain terms if our hair was unacceptable or our shoes not clean. She addressed us all as Miss This or Miss That, almost never using our Christian names. Working in the stalls was the hardest job. We had to eyeball every ticket produced at the door and show the patron to the correct area. People would be coming in and out all evening and we had to keep a watchful eye out to see that the two-and-sixers didn't plonk themselves down in the dearer seats after a trip to the toilet or the ice cream kiosk. If there was a full house, the usherettes had to help with ice cream sales. We had to put a tray round our necks, trot down the aisle and stand in front of the screen, while the engineers in the control room enjoyed themselves by shining the spotlight on us. I hated that part with a passion. A busy night in the circle guaranteed a five pound weight loss, running up and down the stairs from the front of the circle to the 'nose bleed' section right at the top. The mezzanine, for which seats cost 4s 6d – only well-off patrons could afford them – was the easiest area to work, apart from the lift and cloakroom. If we were operating the lift and an important guest arrived we were hauled off the lift so the doorman could operate it. We worked six nights a week; one thirty-minute break each night. On Saturdays we started at 5 p.m. and finished at 10.30 p.m. Nobody had Saturday night off. For all that we earned between £2 and £3 a week. On Sundays we started at 2.30 p.m., when we practised the fire drill. 'Stand by your exits', the manager would shout. Then he came on stage, gave his little speech about vacating the building and we would fling open our exit door, yelling at the top of our voice: 'This way out please. This way out.' If we did not shout loud enough, we were reprimanded the next day.

When the Paramount opened on Oxford Street, a hundred yards away – on the corner of Great Bridgewater Street – was the Hippodrome Theatre. On the site since 1904, it occasionally showed films, one of the most notable being Alfred Hitchcock's first talkie *Blackmail* in December 1929.

In 1935 Bernstein Theatres Ltd, owners of the Granada cinema circuit, bought the Hippodrome. It was to be their first large theatre in the North of England. Architects William T. Benslyn and James Morrison designed the new picture house, which involved demolishing about two thirds of the old theatre; work was completed in seven months, three months less than the expected time. The picture house, to be called the Granada, was set to open on 21 October 1935.

A month before the opening of the Granada, it was announced that the venue had been sold to Gaumont-British, one of the UK's biggest cinema chains and was to be called the Gaumont.

The Odeon had, for five years, been Manchester's most magnificent picture palace, but the Gaumont, with interior design by Theodore Komisarjevsky, surpassed it. The building's outstanding feature was a foyer which ran the whole length of the theatre frontage, with a bar called the Long Bar. In keeping with the importance of the occasion, Gaumont-British pulled out all the stops for the opening. The ceremony was performed by Jessie Matthews, then one of Gaumont-British and the UK's biggest stars, and her husband, Sonnie Hale.

The opening night audience enjoyed an evening of fine entertainment. There was a 'Beauty Parade', Stanley Tudor played the mighty Wurlitzer organ, and the film chosen for showing was a 'big' one: Hitchcock's superb *The 39 Steps*, starring Manchester-born Robert Donat and lovely Madeleine Carroll. An instant success, the Gaumont benefited from clever programming and crafty advertising – 'I'll see you in the Long Bar' was a prominent feature in the adverts.

The Gaumont's success continued into the 1940s and the Second World War, when American GIs, as well as some ladies of dubious reputation, frequented the Long Bar. In the early 1940s Gaumont-British was absorbed into the Rank Organisation, and its cinemas, including Manchester's Gaumont, became part of Rank. Access to some of the best British films (as well as product from Twentieth Century Fox, Paramount and Universal), its prominent site on Oxford Street, and the fact that it was a romantic venue for a night out, ensured the Gaumont good audiences into the 1950s. Moreover, with two picture palaces within yards of each other on the street, Rank had a stranglehold on film entertainment in Manchester city centre.

Most of those interviewed for this book remembered the Gaumont affectionately as 'a great night out' and spoke about the interludes on the organ before the film programme began. In February 1954 the Gaumont became the second Manchester picture house to be equipped to show CinemaScope; Twentieth Century Fox's second CinemaScope film *How to Marry a Millionaire*, starring Marilyn Monroe, Betty Grable and Lauren Bacall, played there. In 1958 the Gaumont's place as Manchester city centre's leading picture house was strengthened when Rank installed a 70mm screen for showing Rodgers and Hammerstein's *South Pacific*, which opened in Manchester just a week after its London premiere, with star Mitzi Gaynor in attendance. Margaret Back, who worked as an usherette at the Odeon, recalls:

> We got an occasional perk of the job. A memorable one was free tickets to the premiere of *South Pacific* at the Gaumont, which my friend Anne and I were delighted to receive. We were just in time to witness Mitzi Gaynor's arrival at the 'Front of House'.

South Pacific ran for two years and two months at the Gaumont – a fantastic achievement – and was succeeded by other 70mm 'biggies' like *The Alamo*, *Spartacus*, *El Cid* and *55 Days at Peking*, all looking marvellous on that giant screen. Seeing pictures at that beautiful venue was, for many people, the cinematic experience of a lifetime.

In 1965 *The Sound of Music* began a two and a half year run at the Gaumont. This author, who had no great liking for Julie Andrews as an actress, was persuaded by my wife to see it a few days after it opened. The antiseptic Miss Andrews was ideal casting as the reluctant nun, though I preferred Eleanor Parker, cast in the thankless role of 'The Baroness' – but even I was astonished by the length of the film's run at the Gaumont.

The Gaumont continued as a showplace for 'big' movies into the 1970s, until Rank decided to twin the Odeon. The twinned cinema opened on 19 January 1974. A week later, Manchester cinema-goers were angered to see press adverts announcing a farewell concert for the Gaumont's Wurlitzer organ. That took place on Sunday 27 January and was recorded by the BBC. A week later, appalled and angry cinema-goers read that the Gaumont was to close on Monday 28 January. Rank wasted no time in getting rid of what was arguably Manchester's finest picture house, whose closing programme was a double bill of *The Graduate* and *Midnight Cowboy*. The building later became a nightclub called 'Rotters' and, when that closed in 1991, was demolished to provide a car park. Today the site is occupied by an office block. Older cinema-goers can only look with sadness at the results of Rank's vandalism – and mourn the loss of Manchester's beautiful and much missed Gaumont.

From the mid-1930s, Manchester had two news theatres on Oxford Street. The Tatler News Theatre occupied a site on Whitworth Street West, at the bottom of the approach to Oxford Road Station. From 1911 the site had been occupied by Manchester Electric Theatres, then by the Whitworth Street Electric Theatre, and later a silent cinema called the Majestic. That was replaced by a furnishing business called Page's and the building was eventually demolished.

In 1934, Times Theatres Ltd, Liverpool, commissioned a new picture house on the site; this, the Tatler News Theatre, opened in May 1935. News theatres were popular in the 1930s and the war years, showing one-hour programmes of travel films, cartoons and newsreels. Patrons could enter at any time during the programme, which made them popular venues.

Programmes at the Tatler started at 2 p.m., with staff coming in between noon and 2 p.m. to clean the premises. The Tatler, showing Fox-Movietone News, operated successfully into the 1950s. However, when the very latest news became available to people in their own homes, via television, news theatres lost out. The Tatler soldiered on till September 1959, before closing for two years. It reopened, in November 1961, as the Manchester Tatler Classic, showing Billy Wilder's Oscar-winning *The Apartment*.

The Classic, as it came to be known, operated throughout the 1960s with programmes of past Hollywood pictures – often coupled in very attractive double bills – as well as European pictures. This author remembers taking his wife there to see the French film *Hiroshima Mon Amour*, which left her distinctly underwhelmed.

As audiences continued to fall, the Classic began to feel the cold, and closed on 31 May 1969 – only to reopen the very next day as the Tatler Cinema Club, showing, to quote its publicity, 'uncensored films, like uncensored plays'. What that meant, in fact, was that if you became a member, you could see – uncut – the more explicit movies from the Continent, which, if shown in ordinary cinemas, had censor cuts and X certificates.

Towards the end of the 1970s, the Tatler Cinema Club really plumbed the depths, with striptease on stage. Its demise came on 15 November 1979. It reopened the next day, once again as the Classic, now showing pictures which had censor approval but were still porn movies – with titles like *Danish Dentist on the Job!* In less than two years it closed again, on 15 August 1981; this time, in spite of an abortive attempt to start the Penthouse Cine Club, showing sex movies, the venue seemed finished.

There was, however, a dramatic development in its life in 1985. The new owners of Shaw's Furniture Stores, a triangular-shaped building on the opposite corner of the station approach from the Tatler, decided to turn it into an arts complex, with two cinemas, a gallery, a bookshop

The main cinema of the Cornerhouse complex in 2009.

and a café. Then they had the brilliant idea of taking over the derelict Tatler building and making that the third and largest cinema in the complex. Thus Cornerhouse was born. It opened on 11 October 1985 with *Insignificance* in Cinema 2 and *Diva* in Cinema 3. Four days later, Cinema 1 (the old Tatler) opened with Luc Besson's *Subway*. In 2009, nearly a quarter of a century after its opening, Cornerhouse is still going strong. It is the only survivor, as a picture house, from the many which populated the city centre in the boom years of cinema. One hopes it will long continue.

Less than a year after the opening of the Tatler News Theatre, Jacey Cinemas opened another news theatre – not more than 200 yards away – at 16 Oxford Street, almost directly opposite the Paramount. Jacey called it the Manchester News Theatre, and its one-time projectionist, Fred Baldwick, later became its manager. Its typically news theatre programming – travel film, cartoon, news – made it a popular venue for people who worked in the area and perhaps fancied a show before going home.

The Manchester News Theatre stayed in business for some thirty-two years, till 1967. Then, on 30 September 1967, Jacey decided it had to close. Just two weeks later the building reopened, this time as the Manchester Film Theatre – a branch of the British Film Institute, which had long wanted a showcase in central Manchester. Paul Rotha, who had made a sixty-minute film about Manchester called *A City Speaks*, attended the opening with his wife (the former actress Constance Smith), as did Sir William Goldsmith, Chairman of the BFI. The opening film was the 1935 French classic *La Kermesse Héroïque*.

For the next five and a half years the Manchester Film Theatre provided excellent entertainment for discerning picture-goers, ranging from the past glories of Hollywood, through the best of British cinema, to the fine pictures which were being produced all over the world by then. The facilities for showing films were second to none. They could be shown in the form in which they had been made – Academy ratio (4x3) widescreen (1.85:1) scope (2.35:1) and even 70mm. One of the best cinematic experiences of this author's life was seeing Nicholas Ray's *King of Kings* there, its stunning Technicolor/Super Technirama photography shown in the correct 70mm ratio on the vast screen.

Amazingly, Manchester – careless of how lucky it was to have such a picture house in the city centre – failed to support the Manchester Film Theatre. The BFI kept it going until April 1973, but then took the decision to close. It would be twelve years before Manchester centre had a comparable venue – the three-screen Cornerhouse, which is also supported by the BFI.

Four months after the closure, the cinema reopened – first as the Film Theatre and then as the Jacey Film Theatre, still trying to bring classy film entertainment to Manchester. That effort lasted just one month, then the name became the Cameo and the programmes nose-dived into luridly-titled sex films and horror movies. In school holidays the Cameo showed Disney pictures, but the display cases outside still carried the legend: 'We are not able to show you any stills because of the explicit content of today's programme,' which must have puzzled parents taking their kids to see *Lady and the Tramp*! The Cameo somehow survived for eight years, finally closing on 22 October 1981. The building was later demolished.

The final picture house to open in the city centre in the twentieth century was a four-screen complex – Studios 6, 7, 8 and 9 – opened by the Star Group in December 1972. This gave the group nine screens in central Manchester, since it owned Studios 1 to 5 on Oxford Road. The new complex, built at a cost of £130,000, was in the lower ground floor area of New Deansgate House, with its entrance and display cases for the four screens on Deansgate itself. The opening programmes were encouraging. Studio 6 had *Under Milk Wood* – a screen adaptation of Dylan Thomas' radio play, starring Elizabeth Taylor, Richard Burton, Peter O'Toole and Glynis Johns. Studio 7 showed the acclaimed French film *Le Genou de Claire* (*Claire's Knee*), Studio 8 *McCabe and Mrs Miller* and Studio 9 the Neil Simon comedy *Plaza Suite*, starring Walter Matthau.

This author waited four years before paying his one and only visit to the complex in 1976. The film was Derek Jarman's *Sebastiane* – unusual because the dialogue was entirely in Latin, though not Latin which I, a Latin teacher, could decipher, thus having to resort to subtitles. The film had achieved some notoriety because of its homoerotic content, which – even with its full-frontal male nudity – was pretty harmless, and certainly nothing to get hot under the collar about. Moreover, the studio in which the film was screened was tiny, making the experience little different from viewing in one's own living room. Studios 6 to 9 lasted sixteen years until 1 June 1988. Then Cannon, which had taken them over from the Star Group, added their closure to the closures of the two Deansgate cinemas and the five-screen complex on Oxford Road, which had already gone. Cannon ran Rank a close second in the vandalism stakes.

Other titles published by The History Press

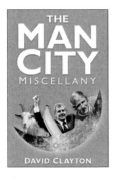

The Man City Miscellany
DAVID CLAYTON

The Man City Miscellany is packed with lists, statistics, tables, song lyrics, quotes and facts – such as the name of Clive Allen's dog, and the meaning behind the 'Invisible Man' the City fans sing about. From club record holders to bizarre goal celebrations, and from peculiar player nicknames to the ups and downs of City's chequered history, this is the only trivia book a Blues fan could ever need.

978 0 7509 4834 0

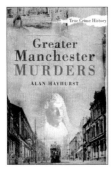

Greater Manchester Murders
ALAN HAYHURST

This book details some of the most notorious murders in the history of Greater Manchester. They include the case of notorious cat burglar, Charlie Peace, who killed 20-year-old PC Nicholas Cook, and only confessed when he had already been sentenced to death for another murder; William Robert Taylor, whose young daughter was killed in a boiler explosion and who later murdered a bailiff as well as his three remaining children; and John Jackson, who escaped from Strangeways Gaol by killing a prison warder.

978 0 7509 5091 6

Hanged at Manchester
STEVE FIELDING

For decades the high walls of Manchester's Strangeways Prison have contained some of England's most infamous criminals. They include Dr Buck Ruxton, who butchered his wife and maid; Walter Rowland, hanged for the murder of a prostitute and the only man to occupy the condemned cell at Strangeways twice; and Oldham teenager Ernie Kelly, whose execution almost caused a riot outside the prison. Also included are the stories behind scores of lesser-known criminals: poisoners, spurned lovers, cut-throat killers, and many more.

978 0 7509 5052 7

Manchester in the '70s
CHRIS MAKEPEACE

Featured here along with street scenes of the city centre and suburbs are images of people, buildings, transport, events and a number of sites which have changed beyond recognition. Most of the photographs included in this book were taken by the author and have never been published before. They are supplemented by posters and adverts to capture the true flavour of the decade. *Manchester in the '70s* is sure to stir feelings of nostalgia in anyone who lived or worked in the city during this fascinating decade.

978 0 7509 4615 5

Visit our website and discover thousands of other History Press books.
www.thehistorypress.co.uk